NEPAL

WHERE THE GODS ARE YOUNG

Asia House Gallery, New York City
Seattle Art Museum
Los Angeles County Museum of Art

NEPAL

WHERE THE GODS ARE YOUNG

by Pratapaditya Pal

The Asia Society

IN ASSOCIATION WITH JOHN WEATHERHILL, INC.

Nepal: Where the Gods Are Young is the catalogue of an exhibition shown in Asia House Gallery in the fall of 1975 as an activity of The Asia Society, to further greater understanding between the United States and the peoples of Asia.

An Asia House Gallery publication

Library of Congress Catalogue Card Number: 75–769
ISBN: 0–87848–045–5

This project is supported by a grant from the National Endowment for the Arts, Washington, D.C., a Federal Agency.

14. Bodhisattva Maitreya; ninth century
Gilt copper with paint; H. 26 in. (frontispiece)

Contents

Foreword

THE ASIA SOCIETY is pleased to present this exhibition, "Nepal: Where the Gods are Young," in association with the Los Angeles County Museum of Art. We have borrowed the services of its Curator of Indian and Islamic Art, Dr. Pratapaditya Pal, who has chosen these objects and written this catalogue. Once again, we are deeply indebted to the National Endowment for the Arts for their generous grant to help cover some of our organizing costs.

This is the second time Asia House Gallery has benefited from Dr. Pal's expertise and scholarship. He first shared his talents with us in 1969 when he organized the exhibition, "The Art of Tibet." From what he wrote then, and reemphasizes here, we see the close affinity between the arts of Tibet and Nepal, and in that sense, the exhibitions themselves are allied. There is an even closer relationship between this display and Stella Kramrisch's pioneering "Art of Nepal" exhibition which she organized for The Asia Society in 1964.

That one Nepal exhibition could lead to another in so short a time is especially significant. Dr. Pal has enlarged upon the earlier exhibition and presents a continuing study of the character of the art. He also gives additional information about its iconography and is able to build further on Dr. Kramrisch's chronology. Although both scholars acknowledge Nepal's debt to India for its underlying religious philosophies and for its art forms, each is impressed by the unique quality of the Nepali expression. Dr. Pal's striking observation from which the title of the exhibition is drawn concerns the quality of youthfulness in the art. The "immortal adolescents" who are the deities of Nepal give these objects their particular and distinct style. With Dr. Pal's conclusion, an all too familiar fact emerges regarding the present condition of the art. He writes of the loss of aesthetic vision that has recently occurred in Nepal. We must therefore appreciate these works with the sad knowledge that yet another art tradition is beginning to die.

In his acknowledgments, Dr. Pal makes two points which are in need of further emphasis because they refer to essential aspects of the history of Asia House Gallery. He mentions the stimulus of the earlier exhibition, in the way it brought about new activity among collectors. This fact was especially well illustrated by an interview which appeared in a recent issue of *Arts of Asia*. It was conducted by Dr. Pal with Jack Zimmerman, whose collection is well represented here. Mr. Zimmerman spoke of his experience in our galleries in 1964 in the following way: "I sort of wandered into the Asia House Gallery almost by accident, and lo and behold, within months, I was collecting Nepalese art . . . That's where my interest began. It was the Asia House show that did it." Such a statement suggests something of the broad influence the Gallery has had during its brief history on the understanding and appreciation of Asian art.

Dr. Pal's second point, the dedication of this book to my predecessor, Gordon B. Washburn, is directly related. Mr. Washburn was chiefly responsible for the programs that brought about this great expansion of our knowledge. The many exhibitions he mounted for the Gallery have always been informative and deeply satisfying to us all. To me, they have now become inspirations.

Allen Wardwell
Director, Asia House Gallery

Acknowledgments

IN 1964 THE FIRST international exhibition of the art of Nepal was organized for Asia House Gallery by Dr. Stella Kramrisch. At that time Nepal and its culture were hardly known in the West. And yet, a decade later when, at the invitation of Gordon B. Washburn, I agreed to organize the present exhibition, I was amazed to find how wide the selection was, even when I limited myself to American collections. In a sense this is a tribute to Dr. Kramrisch's exhibition, which inspired so many new private collectors of Nepali art. Indeed, making a limited selection was not an easy task, and I would particularly like to extend my thanks to all the collectors and curators who have always been cheerfully cooperative.

At The Asia Society in New York I am especially indebted to Virginia Field and Sarah Bradley for their patience and fortitude both with the temperamental process of selection and with the editing of the manuscript. At Los Angeles I would like to express my gratitude to the Board of Trustees of the Museum where I work for allowing me to participate in the exhibition with The Asia Society. It is also a matter of great pleasure to acknowledge the help I have received at the Museum from many colleagues, in particular from Virginia Dofflemeyer, Miki Holiver, Cathy Glynn, and Rochelle Yeker.

Finally, I would like to dedicate this book to Gordon B. Washburn without whose imagination and devotion interest in the arts of Asia in New York City would have languished even during the period when the entire country was witnessing a remarkable expansion of interest in Asian culture in general.

Pratapaditya Pal
Curator of Indian and Islamic Art
Los Angeles County Museum of Art

Lenders to the Exhibition

Asian Art Museum of San Francisco; The Avery Brundage Collection
Mr. and Mrs. Douglas J. Bennet, Jr.
Dr. Edwin Binney, 3rd
Mrs. George H. Bunting
The Cleveland Museum of Art
Denver Art Museum
Mr. Stephen T. Eckerd
Dr. Samuel Eilenberg
Mr. and Mrs. John Gilmore Ford
Mr. Ben Heller
Los Angeles County Museum of Art
The Metropolitan Museum of Art
Mr. and Mrs. Eric D. Morse
Museum of Fine Arts, Boston
Mr. and Mrs. Frank W. Neustatter
The Newark Museum
Pan-Asian Collection
Dorothy and Ernst Payer
Mr. and Mrs. John D. Rockefeller 3rd
The St. Louis Art Museum
Seattle Art Museum
Mr. James D. Thornton
Dr. Claus Virch
Mr. Paul F. Walter
Doris Wiener
Mr. and Mrs. Jack Zimmerman

Introduction

I GODS AND GODDESSES

ACCORDING TO INDIAN MYTHOLOGY, the gods and goddesses, especially those of the Hindu pantheon, inhabit the vast and lofty mountain ranges in the north of the subcontinent, known as the Himalayas. The Kingdom of Nepal is situated almost in the heart of these mountains.

The ethnic composition of Nepal is varied and complex, but the people responsible for creating the majority of the objects included in this exhibition are known as Newars. Concentrated primarily in the Kathmandu valley, which has remained the cradle of Nepali culture for well over two thousand years, the Newars were very likely among the earliest settlers in the area. Sometime around the third century of the Christian era, however, a branch of the Licchavis of India moved into the valley from the present state of Bihar and conquered the local population. The Licchavis consolidated their power, introduced elements of Indian culture, and are known to have ruled until at least the end of the eighth century, if not later. In the year 879 A.D., King Rāghavadeva founded a new era which has come to be known as the Newari era. Although Rāghavadeva may also have been a Licchavi, there is no certainty about this and until we learn more about the dynastic relationships of the kings, the period between 800 and 1200 A.D. may be tentatively characterized as the post-Licchavi period. From 1200 A.D. until the mid-eighteenth century, all the names of the ruling monarchs include the title *malla* and hence this period is identified as the Malla period of Nepali history. In 1768–69 the valley was conquered by Prithivi Narayan Shah from Gorkha in western Nepal and one of his descendents still rules the kingdom.

Throughout its history, Nepal has maintained a close cultural relationship with India. Indian mythological traditions and aesthetic norms have been openly accepted by the people of Nepal, sometimes unchanged, and at other times modified to suit their own religious and artistic needs. Many of the images included here show significant iconographic variations that cannot always be explained in terms of Indian texts. The majority of the Nepali deities, however, entered the secluded Himalayan kingdom from India and essentially retained their Indian forms. Partly because of the diminutive size of the valley.and partly because of the attitude of the people, religious life in the Kathmandu Valley has always been characterized by tolerance and a syncretic spirit. Buddhist and Brahmanical gods have coexisted in comfort and harmony and the average man is often not aware of the sectarian distinction between the deities of the various sects. Thus, Durgā, as Bhagavatī, and the Mother goddesses are venerated universally, as is the god of auspiciousness, Gaṇeśa (No. 90). Like Śiva, Lokeśvara, the Bodhisattva *par excellence*, is a national god, and in the form of Matsyendranātha is worshipped by both Hindus and Buddhists. Perhaps the most classic expression of this attitude of synthesis is revealed in the concepts of Bhairava and Mahākāla. Both names originally signified the angry manifestation of Śiva as the great god of time (Kāla). Subsequently, the name Mahākāla came to be used almost exclusively by the Buddhists, while Bhairava was favored by the Hindus. Their forms, however, are so similar that it is often difficult even for qualified priests and iconographers to distinguish them. One can therefore, well imagine why the ordinary devotee regards all such images loosely as those of Mahākāla. In this exhibition, the unique representation of a bronze shrine of Bhairava (No. 64), where both the Buddhist stupa and the Śaiva linga are included, provides another example of the Nepalis' readiness to combine Buddhist and Brahmanical forms. Perhaps this is what the seventh-century Chinese pilgrim Hsüan-tsang had in mind when he observed that in Nepal the temples of the Hindus and the Buddhists touch one another.

With a few exceptions, virtually every object included in this exhibition either portrays a deity or is associated with one. Whether cast or painted, the majority served as icons to be venerated by the devotee to whom the image was a "live" symbol of a deity rather than just a work of art to be admired in a showcase or on a wall. Because an icon is considered a living entity, it is continuously bathed, clothed (see No. 12), fed and put to sleep—in other words, treated in a very mundane fashion exactly as a family member would be—hence the effaced condition of many of the bronzes. Almost every painting includes a scene of ritual anointment (*abhisheka*), a ceremony which in effect invites the spirit of the deity to descend and reside in the image. This intimate relationship between an image and the person for whom the artist created the image is all too often overlooked today even by the most ardent admirers and aesthetes.

A glance at the illustrations will make it apparent that whether Hindu or Buddhist, benign or angry, rarely—if ever—is a deity portrayed as an elderly person. Indeed, the concepts of old age and death seem to have been perpetually banished from the idealized world of art. Even when a historical event such as the death of the Buddha is depicted (No. 3), the Buddha is portrayed as he might have looked when he preached his first sermon in the deer park at Sarnath some forty years earlier. Or again, when the goddess Durgā is shown destroying Mahishāsura, there is no attempt to portray the agonies of death. In one instance (No. 73), the victim seems totally oblivious of the mortal wound he has suffered, and in another (No. 74), the representation is an almost surrealistic caricature. In either case the goddess is the epitome of divine serenity and youthful charm.

As will be apparent from the textual descriptions quoted below, this insistence on the agelessness of the deity does not reflect the artist's whimsical preference but was dictated by theological injunctions. For example, in most descriptions of the Brahmanical god Vishṇu, the devotee is constantly reminded of the god's radiance, bright as the sun's rays or a thousand moons; of his smooth complexion, like a water-laden cloud or the dark autumn cloud; or of his serene appearance, as fresh as the morning dew.[1] He is also to be portrayed as tall, sturdy, bejewelled and crowned like a king. Even more explicit are the descriptions of the Buddhist goddess Tārā. In one text she is represented as wearing many ornaments (*nānālaṁkāravatī*), charmingly youthful and endowed with fresh, blossoming breasts (*abhinavayauvanodbhinnakuchabhārā*).[2] Elsewhere we are told that she is in the prime of youth and is twice eight years old. Indeed, there is a general insistence upon the fact that the goddesses should be depicted as young women sixteen years of age. This emphasis on youth is evident in the descriptions of women in Sanskrit poetry as well.

Looking at the elegant sculptures of Pārvatī (No. 69) or of Maitreya (No. 14), it is difficult to imagine, however, that an artist could have created such beautiful forms simply with the help of iconometric injunctions and without an intimate knowledge of the human body. Similar thoughts must have provoked the fourth-century Indian poet Kālidāsa to compose the following verse:

> Who was the artificer at her creation?
> Was it the moon, bestowing its own charm?
> Was it the graceful month of spring, itself
> Compact with love, a garden full of flowers?
> That ancient saint there, sitting in his trance,
> Bemused by prayers and dull theology
> Cares naught for beauty: how could he create
> Such loveliness, the old religious fool?[3]

Although the devotee regarded the images essentially as spiritual symbols, the forms of the figures do not reflect a negation of the world of senses. On the contrary, like his Indian counterpart, the Nepali artist also emphasized the physical, and hence sensuous, beauty of the gods and goddesses. Few artistic traditions have combined physical desire and spiritual grace in portraying a divine image as successfully as those of India and of the cultures that derived from the Indian civilization. Wherever the Indian aesthetic models have prevailed, such as in Nepal, Tibet, Indonesia, or Cambodia, the artists have never conceived their gods and goddesses as disembodied spirits, but have created forms that are both sensually appealing and spiritually enthralling. Thus, even if Sambara and Vajravārāhī (No. 32) symbolize spiritual values, their embrace is unabashedly passionate.

Apart from the fact that the gods and goddesses, whether Buddhist or Hindu, are shown as perennially youthful, it will be evident that the same aesthetic standards have been applied consistently, irrespective of sectarian differences. Except for their iconographic peculiarities, there is very little formal difference, for example, between Indra (No. 87) and a Bodhisattva (No. 21), between Śiva (No. 59) and Mañjuśrī (No. 22), or between Pārvatī (No. 69) and Tārā (No. 39). Indeed, the artists have frequently employed the same figurative type, especially for the goddesses that are shown accompanying their consorts. Of course, this often makes it difficult to distinguish these figures if they have been removed from their original context, particularly as, in most such icons, the goddess holds a lotus, which is a ubiquitous symbol of beauty and grace.

It has already been stressed that the gods and goddesses portrayed in Nepali art originated in India. Often, however, only the basic concept was borrowed and the Nepali artists created new iconographic types not familiar in India. Moreover, the Nepali theologians displayed a predilection for certain iconographic forms which better served their own religious needs.

Among the Brahmanical deities, Śiva, Vishṇu, and Durgā are equally popular, although Śiva, in the form of Paśupatinātha, is the national god of the country. Of all the forms of Śiva, those of Umā-Maheśvara (No. 59) and Bhairava (No. 65) are undoubtedly the favorite manifestations. In the Umā-Maheśvara images, the Nepali sculptors have always emphasized the harmonious conjugal relationship between Śiva and his consort. On the other hand, the Bhairava or angry aspect of Śiva was created essentially to instill fear in the devotee. Of the Vaishṇava rites, the one known as *ananta-vrata* holds a special fascination for the Nepalis. Most Vaishnava paintings (see Nos. 80, 81) seem to have been dedicated in honor of this rite and invariably include the form of the serpent Ananta-nāga, which often serves as Vishṇu's parasol or couch (No. 80). It may be noted that the Nepalis have been particularly fascinated by the form of the recumbent Vishṇu since at least the sixth century.

The cult of the goddess Durgā is popular with all Nepalis. She is known generically as Bhagavatī and her temples are numerous. Frequently the goddess is worshipped in the form of an undressed stone, an aniconic object of devotion that obviously survives from neolithic cultures. When represented in her iconic form, she is shown killing either the wicked Mahishāsura or the demons Chaṇḍa and Muṇḍa. She is also worshipped in many tantric forms, the most popular of which are Chāmuṇḍā (also known as Dakshiṇakālī) and Guhyakālī (Nos. 71, 72). Since no image of Guhyakālī has so far come to light in India, it is very likely that she is a Nepali creation.

Of the other Brahmanical deities, special mention must be made of Indra (No. 87). Once the most powerful god of vedic Aryans, Indra subsequently came to occupy a rather insignificant position in the Brahmanical pantheon. In ancient India, however, the festival honoring Indra was celebrated with great pomp and ceremony by kings and commoners alike. The festival is still observed in Nepal and the occasion is highlighted by processions carrying images of Indra through the streets. The majority of these images are made of metal and wood, and the iconic type, to the author's knowledge, is unique to Nepal.

Buddhism, too, is characterized by many unusual cults and forms that appear to be peculiarly local. What Śiva is to the Hindus, the Bodhisattva Avalokiteśvara, commonly known as Lokeśvara, is to the Buddhists. Indeed, more Nepali bronzes portray the classic image of Avalokiteśvara holding a lotus than that of any other Hindu or Buddhist deity (see No. 15). Although the cult of Lokeśvara originated in India, it has acquired a peculiar flavor in Nepal. Among the many forms of Lokeśvara which do not seem to have been widely current in India, if they were known at all, the most popular are those of Amoghapāśa Lokeśvara and Chintāmaṇi Lokeśvara (Nos. 18–20). In both bronzes and paintings these two manifestations are portrayed almost as frequently as the Bodhisattva's simplest form.

Of the other Buddhist deities, Vasudhārā seems to have been especially popular, and in view of the fact that she is the goddess of wealth and prosperity this popularity is not difficult to understand. In neither Indian Buddhist texts nor art have we yet encountered a six-armed image of the goddess. In Nepal, however, she is represented in this form, in both bronzes and paintings, almost as frequently as Avalokiteśvara or his consort Tārā (see Nos. 41–43). That the cult of the six-armed Vasudhārā is at least as old as the eleventh century is evident from a bronze in the exhibition (No. 41). Of the other Buddhist icons, perhaps the most interesting representation is that of the Bodhisattva Vajrapāṇi in which his attribute, the *vajra*, is personified as a dwarf (No. 23). The idea of anthropomorphizing an emblem originated in India and attained some degree of popularity in the Gupta period (300–600 A.D.), but the Nepali artists seem to have developed a special predilection for the concept and they created a number of visually exciting forms (see also No. 24).

Finally, a glance through the illustrations will make it clear that the majority of the deities have two aspects, benign and malevolent. Gods have always been created in the image of man and just as each human being is capable of both kindness and anger, so too are the gods. Only when confronted by evil, however, do they become combative and assume visibly angry forms. In the ultimate analysis the world of gods, as reflected in Hindu and Buddhist mythology, is simply a sublimation of the human experience, with one difference: in the divine drama, death overtakes only the evildoers, while the gods and goddesses, personifying good, remain "immortal adolescents."

II BRONZES

UNTIL THE MIDDLE of the twentieth century the Kingdom of Nepal was virtually closed to Westerners, but the few scholars and travelers permitted to enter the country were invariably impressed by the remarkable metalwork that adorned the temples and palaces in the three main towns of the valley. As early as 1722, Father Desideri, who visited the country for a brief period, found it important to record that the Newars were "clever at engraving and melting metal."[4] Some two centuries later, Percy Brown, an artist and an art-historian, wrote the following encomium after seeing the famous *sundhokā*, or golden doorway, of the Bhatgaon palace.

> A doorway of brick and embossed copper gilt, the richest piece of art work in the whole kingdom, and placed like a jewel flashing innumerable facets in the handsome setting of its surroundings. . . . the artificer of this wonderful doorway has proved in this great work that he was not only a past master of his craft, but a high priest of his cult. . . . As a specimen of man's handicraft it creates a standard whereby may be measured the intellect, artistic and religious, of the old Newars.[5]

Brown's enthusiasm, however, remained confined largely to the world of scholarship. Most books continued to include one or two Nepali bronzes in general surveys of Indian art, but paid scant attention to the validity of the indigenous tradition. The balance was restored for the first time in 1964 with the Asia House exhibition of the art of Nepal organized by Stella Kramrisch.

Over a thousand years before Father Desideri visited Nepal, another foreigner had come to the Kingdom as an ambassador from the court of the T'ang Emperor of China. Like Percy Brown, Wang Hsüan-t'se too was impressed with the profusion and beauty of the metalwork employed in Nepali architecture. His notes formed the basis for the following comments about Nepali metalwork contained in the *New History of the T'ang Dynasty:*

> In the middle of the palace there is a tower of seven stories roofed with copper tiles, balustrade, grilles, columns, beams, and everything therein are set with fine and even precious stones. At each of the four corners of the tower there projects a waterpipe of copper. At the base there are golden dragons which spout forth water. From the summit of the tower water is poured through funnels which finds its way down below, streaming like a fountain from the mouth of the golden Makara.[6]

The palace described in the Chinese sources was very likely the one built by Aṁśuvarman and known as Kailāśakuṭa. More pertinent for us, however, is the reference to extensive use of metal for architectural embellishment. The passage makes it clear that as early as the seventh century, the Nepalis were proficient not only in repoussé work, but also in the art of inlay with semiprecious stones. Little now remains of the architectural accomplishments of the period, but even today the Nepali buildings are striking for their use of metal, especially to cover the roofs, and golden *makaras*, probably similar to those admired by Wang Hsüan-t'se, still adorn the important temples and monasteries.

Considering how ardently Wang Hsüan-t'se admired Nepali craftsmanship, and the fact that he visited Nepal twice, it would be reasonable to assume that he must have taken some souvenirs of his visit back to China. If these were images of Buddhist gods and goddesses, they may have exerted some influence upon contemporary Buddhist sculpture in China. We are more certain, however, of the strong influence of Nepali art on Chinese Buddhist art during the period of the Yüan dynasty in the thirteenth century, and later. The newly converted emperor, Kubilai Khan had requested his Tibetan preceptor, the abbot of the Sakya-pa monastery, to send him an artist to create images for the imperial chapel. The Tibetan abbot turned to his contemporary Nepali monarch, who promptly dispatched a contingent of eighty artists under the leadership of a young man called A-ni-ko. Not only did A-ni-ko achieve great success at the imperial court, but his artistic and iconometric instructions were later codified by one of his disciples, and many of the Buddhist images subsequently created in China followed this manual.

It is also significant for the history of Tibetan art that the Sakya-pa abbot had to seek artists in Nepal to meet the Chinese emperor's demands. Indeed, Tibet's dependence upon the Nepali artistic tradition is evident not only from bronzes but also from paintings. As will be shown later, Nepali artists have been present continuously in Tibet and the influence of Nepali art on that of Tibet has been prolonged and profound.

Like the gods and goddesses, the forms and styles of Nepali sculpture entered the country from India. The bronzes that are here attributed to the Licchavi period of Nepali history (ca. 400–850 A.D.) unquestionably demonstrate the predominant influence of the aesthetic tradition of Gupta India (ca. 300–600 A.D.). The Heller Buddha (No. 1) and the Pan-Asian Vajrapāṇi (No. 23) reveal the same mixture of sensuous charm and spiritual grace that is the hallmark of Gupta sculpture. The proportions reflect mathematical exactitude and the modeling is tempered with almost languorous elegance. Indeed, the Gupta tradition remained valid in Nepal, perhaps because of its geographical seclusion, for a much longer period than in North India. The radiantly beautiful Maitreya of the ninth century (No. 14) or the enchanting Pārvatī (No. 69) of about the same period reveal the enduring influence of the classic style.

It has become axiomatic with modern scholars to assert that post-ninth century Nepali art was strongly influenced by the Pāla art of eastern India. Yet it is curious that the Nepali temples and monasteries have not yielded a single Pāla bronze. On the contrary, several Nepali bronzes have been discovered in India, in and around Nalanda. At any rate, a comparison between Nepali and Pāla bronzes of about the tenth and eleventh centuries completely belies such an assumption.

A glance at the magnificent Padmapāṇi (No. 15), the majestic Indra (No. 87) or even the fourteenth-century Tārā (No. 38) will make it evident that these sculptures owe little or nothing to Pāla bronzes of either Kurkihar or Nalanda. In general, Pāla bronzes have oval faces with sharper features, and display more naturalistic modeling, as well as a conscious attempt to deviate from Gupta models. The Nepali bronzes, on the other hand, have rounder faces with softer features, show less concern with musculature, and remain close to the Gupta models. Moreover, inasmuch as bronzes from the two areas have recognizably distinct patinas and finishes, the technical differences between Nepali and Pāla bronzes are self-evident. As I have said elsewhere, "what is common to both is rather the result of their common heritage, for both the Pāla and Nepali styles are ultimately derived from the Kushāna-Gupta tradition."[7]

Stylistic changes are less easily perceptible in Nepali art than elsewhere, due mainly to the remoteness of the kingdom. Furthermore, the sanctity of an image prevented rapid stylistic mutations, for consistency in appearance was regarded as vital to the continued potency of an image. Archaic and often anomalous survivals, therefore, are not uncommon, which makes the task of the art-historian all the more challenging. Few Nepali bronzes are inscribed or dated. It happens, however, that three of the earliest dated bronzes included in this catalogue (Nos. 41, 55, 79) belong to the eleventh century. With the help of such bronzes and of dated stone sculptures, we are in a far better position today to suggest a relatively secure chronology for Nepali bronzes than was possible even a decade ago.

Despite persistence of Gupta forms, a subtle stylistic change became noticeable in Nepali bronzes after the twelfth century. There was henceforth a greater exuberance in ornamentation and the modeling was not always as full and opulent. The faces began to assume a pronounced Mongoloid shape and the features were not defined as sharply and articulately as in the earlier figures. After the sixteenth century the style became mannered and introverted, and the creative force abandoned the form to take refuge in ornamentation and embellishment. Nonetheless, it must be kept in mind that while in most of North India the bronze tradition began languishing after the twelfth century, in Nepal it remained vital and even creative well into the eighteenth century. Indeed, the majority of the surviving Nepali bronzes belong to the present millennium.

Bronzes created between the fourteenth and seventeenth centuries are perhaps more truly Nepali than the earlier pieces. They are definitely more easily recognizable than contemporary Indian works and reveal far greater technical sophistication. As a matter of fact, most of the tantric bronzes belong to this period and one cannot but be impressed by the sheer technical dexterity of the Newari artists. Whether we admire the monumentality of the Cleveland Mañjuśrī (No. 22), the delicate intricacy of the Boston Sarasvatī (No. 76), the ardent expression of the Nāgarāja (No. 92) or the serene grandeur of Durgā killing Mahishāsura (No. 73), they are all inspired works of a vital tradition that may be said to express a distinctly Nepali *Kunstwollen*.

The unknown Nepali sculptors have also given us some remarkably expressive representations of movement. Many of these bronzes are relatively small (see Nos. 49, 88, 91), but they are nonetheless exciting delineations of graceful postures from the dancer's repertoire. Elegantly simple, they are no less lively and animated than some of the more vigorous tantric forms. Like his Indian counterpart, the Nepali sculptor appears to have been a keen observer of the human body engaged in dancing. When perceptive writers remark that Indian dancing has a sculpturesque quality, they are only underscoring the intimate relationship that has always existed between the forms of dance and sculpture. The bronzes of Nepal express and explore this relationship with unqualified success.

Unlike the images carved in stone or wood, mostly in relief, the majority of the bronzes are free-standing sculptures. Since an image was usually viewed from the front, however, the back was not always as well finished as the front. The bronzes may be either solid or hollow, and the preferred method of casting was the "lost wax," or *cire perdue*, process. It may be mentioned that although we use the term "bronze" to refer to these metal sculptures, they are made mainly of copper. After an image was cast, it was carefully and exquisitely chased to bring out the details of the ornaments, and finally was gilded. In addition to casting, the Newaris are equally proficient in repoussé, or beaten metalwork. In fact, many of the architectural embellishments, such as the glittering roofs and spires that dazzle the eyes of visitors to the Kathmandu valley, are manufactured by the repoussé technique. The eleventh-century Zimmerman plaque of Vishṇu riding on Garuḍa (No. 79) is one of the earliest and finest examples of a repoussé bronze that has come to light.

The use of gold to enhance the magical attraction of a divine image has always had a universal appeal. In Nepal, gilding was applied to most metal images, and often the principal images within the temples were covered with plaques similar to the one in the Zimmerman Collection (No. 79). Moreover, the Newars were inordinately fond of encrusting their gilt images with semiprecious stones—a proclivity that was also adopted by the Tibetans, as may be seen in a richly adorned shrine in the exhibition (No. 13). While the images are the symbols of gods, the shrines and temples are symbolic of paradise. And whether the paradise is that of the Brahmanical Indra or of the Buddhist Tathāgatas, it is always described in terms of gold and precious gems. In speaking of the western paradise of Amitābha, the Buddha declares: "And there, O Ânanda, of the trees made of gold, the flowers, leaves, small branches, branches, trunks and roots are made of gold, and the fruits are made of silver."[8]

III PAINTINGS

BY COMPARISON with the bronzes, the paintings included here exhibit a richer repertoire. While the sculptor was largely restricted to creating icons and ritual objects, the painters could draw upon the vast and varied world of Brahmanical and Buddhist mythology, depicting subjects of narrative interest in addition to images of gods and goddesses. Consequently, we perceive not only a greater diversity of themes in the paintings, but also a wider variety of styles.

Although the Chinese sources testify that the people of Nepal delighted in painting the walls of their houses during the Licchavi period (ca. 400–850 A.D.), the earliest surviving paintings go back only to the eleventh century. These are chiefly manuscript illuminations, executed both on palm-leaf pages and on the wooden covers used to protect the manuscripts. From our two twelfth-century examples (Nos. 44, 56), it will be evident that there is no perceptible stylistic difference between the Buddhist and the Brahmanical illuminations. By far the larger quantity of such manuscripts that have survived is Buddhist, and the illustrations seem to echo distantly the rich and vivid style that was employed in fifth-century India to decorate the Buddhist shrines at Ajanta. Usually the manuscripts illustrate gods and goddesses depicted in a strictly hieratic manner and hence the compositions are both limited and stereotyped. Nonetheless, the delineation is often lively and the figures are modeled with consummate skill, considering their remarkably diminutive size. The emphasis is always on bright masses of primary colors, employed to create contrasting effects.

The tradition of illuminating palm-leaf manuscripts and their covers was also common in the monasteries of eastern India at this time, and it can be postulated that the two traditions were closely related. At the same time, however, a close scrutiny of the illuminations makes it clear that the two styles were quite distinct. The Pāla style of India was far more conservative and illustrative, whereas the Nepali style was usually more expressive and more painterly. Moreover, the Nepali tradition remained vital for a much longer period of time and, therefore, was susceptible to other influences as well.

Far better known among collectors and scholars are the religious icons known as *paṭa* in Sanskrit, *paubhā* in Newari, and *thanka* in Tibetan. Always painted on coarse cotton, these *paubhās* portray both Brahmanical and Buddhist images, although the latter predominate. No study of the technique of painting such *paubhās* has yet been made and all that can be said for the present is that the pigments were mixed with water and that some sort of a gum resin was used as an adhesive. When well preserved these paintings last for centuries, as is evident from the number of early examples included here (Nos. 10, 40, 43).

Although the earliest dated *paubhā* discovered in Nepal is the 1367 mandala of Vasudhārā (No. 43), the brilliantly executed painting of Ratnasambhava in Los Angeles (No. 10) and its companion in Boston must be regarded as the earliest *paubhās* known. Their close stylistic similarity to eleventh- and twelfth-century manuscript illuminations can hardly be questioned. The smaller figures in these *paubhās* have the same diminutive but graceful proportions as those in the illuminations. The compositions are characterized by the same feeling of gentle animation and the pigments have a similarly soft and luminous quality. Although there are many more figures in the *paubhās*, it is evident that the rules of frontality and symmetry are axiomatic in this world of symbols and images.

The basic compositional scheme seen in the twelfth-century Los Angeles *paubhā* (No. 10) remained valid for all future representations of benign deities. Although the style of painting has changed over the centuries, the compositional formula has not. Variations may be noted for mandalas (Nos. 19, 43) and the portrayals of wrathful deities (Nos. 32, 45), but the emphasis is always on visual order, spatial symmetry, and hieratic frontality. The principal difference lies in the overall design: in the mandala, the composition is dominated by the geometric pattern of the mandala itself, while in the icons of wrathful deities, the overpowering motif is the flaming red aureole, or *prabhā*, that occupies much of the painting's background. The central figures in the mandala paintings are usually not much larger than the subsidiary acolytes, whereas in the paintings of angry deities, as in those of benign deities, the principal figures assert their importance in terms of size. Common to all such *paubhās* are a register of ancillary divinities at the top, and another register at the bottom containing portraits of donors and scenes of ritual consecration.

A glance at the paintings, especially the *paubhās*, included here, will also reveal certain other common features that have persisted throughout the ages. As a rule, only the primary colors are employed, and among these red always predominates. Indeed, the Nepali artists seem to have been obsessed with the color red and to have used it with great skill. Moreover, the Nepali red has a very special rich tonality that is clearly distinguishable from the reds used in Indian or Tibetan paintings. This preponderance of red, supported by an intense blue, a deep green, and a bright yellow, imbues the Nepali *paubhās* with unusual warmth and richness. Although there are often subtle variations of shades and tonalities in a given painting, the overall visual impression remains one of strong areas of bold colors contrasting with each other in specific areas of a painting, but blending harmoniously in the total composition.

It need hardly be stressed that in predominantly religious paintings such as these, nature *per se* has no place, except when natural objects have been used as symbols. For example, it was unimportant to the artist whether the lotus, which plays a prominent role as the support of various deities, was true to its natural form. That the artists were keen observers and knew the form and structure of the flower is unquestionable, but since the lotus serves a purely symbolic function in the paintings, they felt free to paint it in variegated colors. Indeed, the emphasis is always on creating richness of detail and on making the overall pattern pleasing to the eye. Thus trees, flowers, thrones, arches, animals, and birds are rendered as decorative symbols. This becomes at once apparent if we look at the superb painting of Tārā at Cleveland (No. 40) or the Śaiva painting in the Ford Collection (No. 57). No one will insist that the artists responsible for the trees in the former or the rocks in the latter led cloistered lives divorced from nature, and yet these objects have been rendered in a delightfully decorative manner that bears little relation to their natural forms.

This obvious delight in visual patterns rather than the desire to imitate the true forms of nature remained dominant even when the artist was called upon to represent narrative subjects. The portrayal of myths and didactic stories is an important aspect of Nepali painting. Commonly such myths are depicted in long narrow scrolls such as the Śaiva scroll (No. 62); sometimes stories are also included in *paubhās* (see Nos. 19, 43). In both instances there is a tendency to divide the story into small segments in a comic-strip fashion. In the *paubhās*, the general practice is to set the scenes within painted frames but, in the scrolls, trees or sections of buildings are often employed to separate the episodes. The depiction is always direct and simple, with no attempt to portray emotions or the dramatic tension of a situation. The representation is almost invariably flat, and there is no conscious effort to convey an illusionistic sense of depth. This remained largely true even after the arrival of Rajput influences from India in the seventeenth century (see Nos. 85, 97). In the Śaiva scroll (No. 62) we encounter both trees and water but, not only are they rendered conceptually, there is no attempt to create even a rudimentary landscape. The language of symbols has not changed over the centuries, only the style of expression is different.

Although the tradition remained conservative in general, stylistic changes or differences were far more emphatic in the case of paintings than in that of bronzes. Even if they are difficult to describe, such changes or differences are easily perceived. One has only to compare the Cleveland Tārā (No. 40) with the Vasudhārā mandala (No. 43), the Vishṇu mandala (No. 80) with the nearly contemporary Śaiva painting (No. 57), or the two *paubhās* of Achala Chaṇḍamahāroshaṇa (Nos. 33, 34) to realize how original and individualistic the different painters were, even though they painted in the same basic tradition. Unfortunately nothing is known of either the artists or the ateliers responsible for these works, despite the fact that some of them are inscribed. Nor are we better informed about the donors who commissioned such works. In exceptional instances, such as in the Cleveland painting of the Preaching Buddha (No. 6), we find the Buddha expounding the doctrine directly to a donor. Although rare, there are a few other examples of images which show the Buddha or a deity blessing or communicating with a devotee (No. 40). One can surmise that in such instances the subject matter was influenced by the wishes of the donor rather than the predilections of the artist. It must be stressed, however, that the donor probably had nothing to do with the manner of representation.

Around 1600, in the town of Bhatgaon (also known as Bhaktapur), there was apparently a particular atelier whose artists developed a distinctive style, seen here in the delightful Śaiva scroll from a private collection (No. 62). No direct antecedents of this style are known. Other, earlier narrative paintings are completely different, and the narrative scenes in the Cleveland "Preaching Buddha" (No. 6), dated 1649 and probably painted in Kathmandu, seem to continue the earlier tradition. The *Nāyikā* folio (No. 97), perhaps also painted at Bhatgaon, but around 1650, is very different, stylistically, from the Śaiva scroll from Bhatgaon, nor does it resemble in manner its near-contemporary, the "Preaching Buddha." Such clearly recognizable stylistic differences are rarely perceptible in the bronzes of a given period.

The first half of the seventeenth century witnessed the influence on Nepali painting of a new stylistic tradition. By the year 1600 the Mughal style had crystallized in the imperial atelier of Akbar and soon radically affected the native Indian tradition of painting, including the Rajput style which evolved in the princely courts of Rajasthan and Central India. That the influences of the Rajput style reached Nepal by the mid-seventeenth century is evident from the *Nāyikā* painting included here (No. 97).

The *Nāyikā* folio, which belongs to a set of eight *Nāyikā* paintings that were bound into an album as a preface to a *Rāgamālā* series, appears to be the earliest example of a secular painting that has come to light in Nepal. Generally, subjects for painting, even those used to decorate secular buildings such as the palaces at Kathmandu and Bhatgaon, were drawn from the rich world of mythology. Both the *Nāyikā* and the *Rāgamālā* paintings reflect a different attitude toward art, one that involves a new kind of aesthetic connoisseurship. Although the *Nāyikā-Rāgamālā* album

97. *Folio From a Nāyikā Series; ca. 1650. Opaque watercolor on paper;* H. 7 1/16 *in.,* W. 5 5/8 *in. (opposite)*

आश्लेषचुंबनशतैःकुसुमादिदानैःप्रेमोलसत्प्रणयकोमलचाटुवाग्भिः
संस्तूयतेप्रियतमेनचयानुरागात्स्वाधीनभर्तृकपरिकीर्तितासा॥

is at present a solitary example, very likely other such paintings were commissioned by seventeenth-century Nepali kings in emulation of their Mughal peers in India.[9]

Hitherto, paper manuscripts had followed the shape and format of the earlier palm-leaf books—long and narrow—and both the size and scope of the illuminations were necessarily limited. In some instances, the long, band-like scroll paintings were imitated on paper in even smaller dimensions. The *Nāyikā* painting not only ushers in a new format with the vertically oriented composition found in western books and canvases, but also introduces the idea of the picture album where each folio is conceived as a separate pictorial composition. Two other similar album leaves that illustrate purely religious subjects, and belong to a later period, are also included in this exhibition (Nos. 74, 85).

Despite the fact that the *Nāyikā* painting was modeled after Rajput originals—very likely of the Mewar school—it is obvious that the Nepali artist was not a blind imitator. On the contrary, he borrowed only the basic compositional idea from his model. The figurative types and decorative motifs, as well as the application of colors, decidedly reflect the aesthetic standards of his native tradition. Moreover, there seems little doubt that the artist was primarily a painter of religious paintings for he quite incongruously placed the entire scene of the lovers on a lotus base of the sort that appears in the *paubhās* (see No. 32).

Far more individualistic was the painter of the *Bhāgavata* series from which two leaves are included here. One of the leaves (No. 85a) shows a composition with an unusual emphasis on architectural views and perspectives. Indeed, the majority of the folios in this series reflect the artist's obsession with architectural compositions, which is so overwhelming that the figures appear to have been included almost incidentally. Equally exuberant is the use of colors that enhance the liveliness of the composition, and compensate for the geometric formality of the architectural elements. By comparison with the other folios in the series, the Los Angeles folio (No. 85b), portraying a celestial landing, is both a refreshing variation and a remarkable *tour de force*. The artist depicted the scene from an aerial vantage point, as if he were watching Krishṇa's arrival from a control tower. Especially attractive is the overall design of the composition with its rigidly geometrical, colorful buildings, pleasantly contrasting with the abstract tortoise-like shape of the green earth.

In contrast to the earlier paintings, whether *paubhās* or scrolls, in these *Bhāgavata* pages the ubiquitous use of a red or a blue background has been dispensed with. Instead, we now have a new formula for the ground: a green, gently undulating field with tufts of black scrubby grass. Obviously, this attempt to add naturalism to the works derives from the Mughal-Rajput tradition. In the Amoghapāśa mandala (No. 19) still further attempts are made to add landscape elements. The formula for such a landscape was actually conceived in the eighteenth century, for narrative scrolls. Long bands of uniformly ascending mountains capped with jagged snowy peaks, resembling stage backdrops, became a popular motif. Although the artists must have seen landscapes in the Mughal-Rajput paintings, their predilection for these snow-topped mountains probably reflected influences from the Pahari and Tibetan traditions. Certainly the cloud patterns commonly seen in later Nepali paintings derive from Tibet. Even though the Nepali artists of the eighteenth century showed an awareness of landscape elements in their paintings, they obviously used these elements to achieve a decorative design rather than a natural setting.

It is evident from both the Amoghapāśa mandala (No. 19) and the considerably earlier manuscript covers (No. 94) that some Nepali artists had also begun to attempt to convey a sense of depth. The narrative scenes in the mandala show a far more convincing spatial relationship between the figures, the architecture and the trees, than do the compositions in earlier works (see No. 62, for example). Very likely such experiments were stimulated by Mughal or Pahari paintings. Indeed, some of the compositions in the Amoghapāśa mandala, where people are shown seated within pavilions, seem to imitate similar compositions in Pahari paintings very closely.

The Mughal influence is more readily perceptible in the portraits of the period. Although the tradition of idealized portraiture in sculpture can probably be traced back to the Licchavi period, the painted portraits, such as those of Pratāpamalla (No. 6), Jitāmitramalla (No. 81), or an unknown king and his guru (No. 94), have been strongly influenced by the contemporary Mughal tradition. The dress of the figures, complete with the sash and the typical dagger known as a *katar*, the strong emphasis on the profile, as well as the comparatively realistic delineation of the features, enhanced by shading, are all elements derived from Mughal portrait paintings. Especially naturalistic are the representations on the manuscript covers, where not only the king, but also the priest and the elephants are painted with consummate skill.

IV NEPAL AND THE ART OF TIBET

IT MUST BE CLEAR from the above discussion that while the Indian aesthetic tradition was the principal source of inspiration for the artists of Nepal, throughout history the Nepali genius has always expressed itself with creative self-assurance. In their turn, the artists of Nepal were largely responsible for molding the Tibetan tradition and even contributing to the Buddhist art of Yüan China. The influence of Nepali art on Tibetan paintings and bronzes was especially strong.

After the eleventh century when the monasteries in India were destroyed, the Tibetans turned increasingly to Nepal not only for spiritual reinforcements, but also for aesthetic inspiration. Tibetan pilgrims who visited the famous monasteries of Nepal must have returned to their country with both bronzes and paintings, which were then copied in Tibet just as the Indian images had been. Far more influential were Nepali artists themselves, who were frequently invited to paint murals in Tibetan monasteries. The fact that the abbot of the Sakya-pa monastery had to send to Nepal for artists to fulfill the request of Kubilai Khan clearly indicates that qualified masters in Tibet were few and far between, even in the fourteenth century. Over a century later when the new monastery was built at Nor, artists from Nepal were invited to paint the murals, and Tibetan texts preserve the names of a large number of Nepali artists who were responsible for painting murals in other and older monasteries in that country. It is well known that the Newar metalsmiths enjoyed a special reputation in Tibet for their extraordinary skill in casting images. Moreover, a mixed community known as Urha—the result of marriages between Newars and Tibetans—has been chiefly responsible for all metal casting in Tibet for centuries. Indeed, a few of the bronzes included in this exhibition may actually have been cast in Tibet by Newari or Urha craftsmen. Despite the fact that it was created in Tibet, the spectacular shrine (No. 13) clearly illustrates the refined and delicate workmanship for which the Newars are famous.

More obviously Nepali, although probably executed in Tibet, are a number of paintings included here. A few of these (Nos. 3, 11), are rendered in a very distinctive style which was labeled as the Nepali manner by Professor Tucci.[10] That they are closely related to the Ratnasambhava painting (No. 10) seems incontestable but, at the same time, their stylistic distinctiveness is equally apparent. One wonders if the style was not evolved in Tibet with strong influences from both Nepali and Indian paintings. The Zimmerman paintings of the Life of the Buddha and of Vajrasattva (Nos. 3, 29) certainly seem to reflect a figurative manner deriving more from eastern Indian manuscript illuminations than Nepali sources, but the lively drawing, the soft modeling of the figures, and the tonality of the colors clearly betray the handiwork of Nepali artists.

The Nepali influence is even more pronounced in the charming paintings of Vajravārāhī (No. 46) and Kurukullā (No. 48). Although some characteristics are peculiarly Tibetan, both paintings use the intense red background that is favored by the Nepali artists. Despite the fact that the monks in the Vajravārāhī painting belong to the Tibetan pantheon, the central representation of the goddess is astonishingly close to the much larger Nepali painting of Vajravārāhī in another private collection (No. 45). Similarly, only the landscape elements in the Kurukullā painting are Tibetan, the basic composition, the crisp through careful drawing and the intensely red flame background are directly derived from paintings such as the Los Angeles Sambara (No. 32). Thus, if these two paintings were not actually painted by Nepali artists in Tibet, as seems likely, they must have been painted by Tibetan artists intimately familiar with the Nepali tradition.

The gods and goddesses are very much alive in Nepal and their images continue to be produced for worship, but the aesthetic vision that created the great works of art discussed here seems to have become blurred, if not altogether myopic. The images that are still fashioned by traditional craftsmen grace the shrines of only the most ardent devotees. "Art" is now the prerogative of artists who look to the industrial West for their ideas and inspiration. In this new aesthetic adventure, the "immortal adolescents" of the Nepali pantheon no longer have a role to play.

---

1. See H. D. Smith (ed.), *Vaiṣṇava Iconography* (Madras, 1969).
2. B. Bhattacharyya, *The Indian Buddhist Iconography*, 2nd ed. (Calcutta, 1958), p. 128.
3. J. Brough, *Poems from the Sanskrit* (Baltimore, 1968), p. 63.
4. D. R. Regmi, *Medieval Nepal* (Calcutta, 1966), vol. II, p. 1009.
5. P. Brown, *Picturesque Nepal* (London, 1912), pp. 71–73.
6. K. P. Jayaswal, "Chronology and History of Nepal," *Journal of the Bihar and Orissa Research Society*, XXII, 3 (1936), pp. 238–239.
7. P. Pal, "The Bronzes of Nepal," *Arts of Asia*, IV, 5 (Sept.–Oct. 1974), p. 34.
8. M. Muller (tr.), "The Larger Sukhâvatî-vyûha" in *Buddhist Mahâyâna Texts*, vol. XLIX, pt. II, (Delhi/Varanasi/Patna, 1955), p. 34.
9. The entire *Rāgamālā* set is now in the collection of the Norton Simon Foundation. For a discussion of the other seven *Nāyikā* folios, see P. Pal, "Eight Heroines from Nepal," *Los Angeles County Museum of Art Bulletin 1974*, XX, 2, pp. 58–63.
10. See P. Pal, *The Art of Tibet* (New York: Asia House Gallery, 1969), p. 131 and no. 1.

In this catalogue, the bronzes and paintings representing the individual deities have been grouped together and placed in chronological order. The first part of the catalogue concerns Buddhist deities, beginning with several Buddha images. Next follow Bodhisattvas, various tantric deities, goddesses, and ritual objects associated with Buddhism. The second part deals with the deities of the Brahmanical pantheon. Images of Śiva in several of his manifestations are followed by an array of goddesses and then by Vishṇu and related deities. Various other celestial beings as well as religious and secular objects associated with Brahmanism complete the catalogue.

Buddhist Art

1. *Buddha Śākyamuni; seventh century*
Gilt copper; H. 19¾ *in. (above)*

2. *Buddha Śākyamuni; ninth century*
Copper alloy; H. 10½ *in. (above right)*

3. *Life of the Buddha; fourteenth century*
Opaque watercolor on cloth; H. 31½ *in.*, W. 23½ *in. (opposite)*

4. *The Temptation of Śākyamuni; dated* 1561
Opaque watercolor on cotton; H. 42¾ *in.*, W. 29¾ *in. (detail above)*

5. *Buddha Śākyamuni; sixteenth century*
Gilt copper; H. 10¾ *in. (above)*

6. *Buddha Preaching; dated* 1649
Opaque watercolor on cloth; H. 43¼ *in.,* W. 32½ *in. (opposite)*

7. *Head of a Buddha Image; seventeenth century*
Gilt copper with paint; H. 9⅞ *in.,* W. 8 *in. (opposite)*

8. *Buddha as the Supreme Healer; fifteenth century*
Opaque watercolor on cloth; H. 20¾ *in.,* W. 17½ *in. (right)*

9. *Tathāgata Akshobhya; tenth-eleventh century*
Copper alloy with traces of gilt; H. 8 *in. (above)*

10. *Ratnasambhava and the Eight Bodhisattvas; twelfth century*
Opaque watercolor on cotton; H. 16⅛ *in.,* W. 13 *in. (opposite)*

11. *A Buddhist Theophany; thirteenth century*
Opaque watercolor and gold on cotton; H. 31½ *in.,* W. 25 *in. (below)*

12. *Dīpaṅkara Buddha; eighteenth century*
Wood and gilt copper; H. *24¼ in. including pedestal (left)*

13. *A Shrine with a Buddha Image; eighteenth century*
Gilt bronze inlaid with semiprecious stones; H. *35 in.,* W. *22 in. (below)*

15. *Bodhisattva Avalokiteśvara; eleventh-twelfth century*
Gilt copper; H. *23½ in. (opposite)*

16. *Eleven-headed Avalokiteśvara; eleventh century*
Gilt copper with traces of polychrome; H. 19⅜ *in. (opposite left)*

17. *Eleven-headed Avalokiteśvara; thirteenth century*
Gilt copper inlaid with semiprecious stones; H. 12⅛ *in. (opposite right)*

18. *Amoghapāśa Lokeśvara; fifteenth century*
Opaque watercolor on cotton; H. 24½ *in.,* W. 21 *in. (above)*

19. *Mandala of Amoghapāśa Lokeśvara; dated* 1867
Opaque watercolor on cotton; H. 44¾ *in.,* W. 35 *in. (opposite)*

20. *Chintāmaṇi Lokeśvara; eighteenth century*
Gilt copper with semiprecious stones; H. 7½ *in.,* W. 4¼ *in. (above)*

21. *A Bodhisattva; thirteenth century*
Gilt copper inlaid with semiprecious stones; H. 19 *in. (below)*

22. *Bodhisattva Mañjuśrī; fifteenth century*
Gilt bronze inlaid with semiprecious stones; H. 30¾ *in. (opposite)*

23. *Bodhisattva Vajrapāṇi; eighth century*
Copper with traces of gilt; H. *7 in.*

24. *Vajrapurusha (?); tenth century*
Gilt copper; H. *5¼ in.*

25. *Bodhisattva Vajrapāṇi; ninth–tenth century*
Gilt copper; H. 8 *in.*

26. *Bodhisattva Vajrapāṇi; twelfth century*
Gilt bronze; H. 10 *in. (above)*

27. *Mahāchakra Vajrapāṇi; fifteenth century*
Gilt bronze with polychrome, inlaid with semiprecious stones; H. 13¼ *in. (opposite)*

28. *Two Embracing Tantric Deities; fifteenth century*
Silver with polychrome; H. 5 *in.* *(illus. p. 46)*

29. *Vajrasattva and Consort; fourteenth century*
Opaque watercolor on cotton; H. *14½ in.,* W. *13 in. (illus. p. 47)*

30. *A Lotus Mandala; eleventh–twelfth century*
Copper alloy cast in several pieces; H. *(closed) 6¼ in.,* W. *(open) 6½ in. (opposite)*

31. *Hevajra; twelfth–thirteenth century*
Copper with traces of gilt; H. *9¾ in. (below)*

32. *Sambara with Consort; ca.* 1500
Opaque watercolor on cotton; H. 54 *in.*, W. 45 *in. (opposite)*

33. *Chaṇḍamahāroshaṇa; sixteenth century*
Opaque watercolor on cotton; H. 34 *in.*, W. 26 *in. (above)*

34. *Chaṇḍamahāroshaṇa; seventeenth century*
Opaque watercolor on cotton; H. 32¼ *in.,* W. 23 *in. (opposite)*

35. *An Angry God; tenth–eleventh century*
Gilt copper with gold paint; H. 15 *in. (above left)*

36. *Tārā; seventh century*
Copper alloy; H. 11⅞ *in. (above right)*

37. *Tārā; eleventh century*
Gilt copper; H. 8 9/16 *in. (left)*

38. *Tārā; fourteenth century*
Gilt copper with semiprecious stones and paint; H. 20 1/4 *in. (opposite)*

39. *Mahāśrī Tārā with Companions; tenth century*
Gilt copper; H. 8 *in. (below)*

40. *Green Tārā; ca.* 1300
Opaque watercolor on cotton; H. 20½ *in.,* W. 17 *in. (opposite)*

41. *Vasudhārā; dated* 1082
Gilt copper inlaid with semiprecious stones; H. 8½ *in. (above)*

42. *Vasudhārā; twelfth century*
Bronze inlaid with semiprecious stones; H. 19 *in. (right)*

43. *Mandala of Vasudhārā; dated 1367*
Opaque watercolor on cotton; H. 40¾ *in.,* W. 34½ *in. (detail above)*

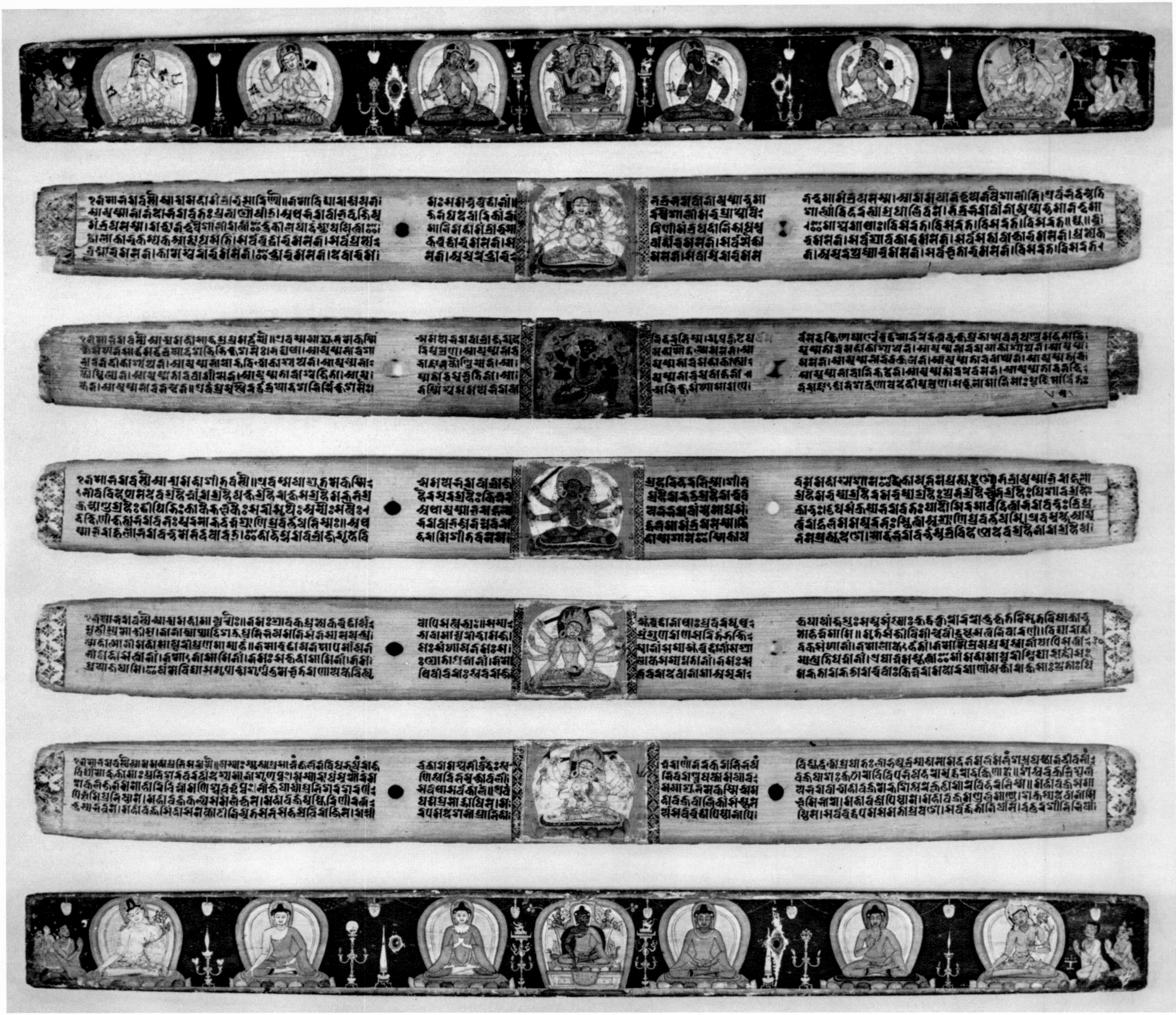

44. *Two Covers and Five Folios of a Pañcharakshā Manuscript; dated* 1138
Ink and color on wood and palm leaves; Covers: H. 2½ *in.*, W. 22½ *in.*
Leaves: H. 2¼ *in.*, W. 21⅞ *in. (detail above)*

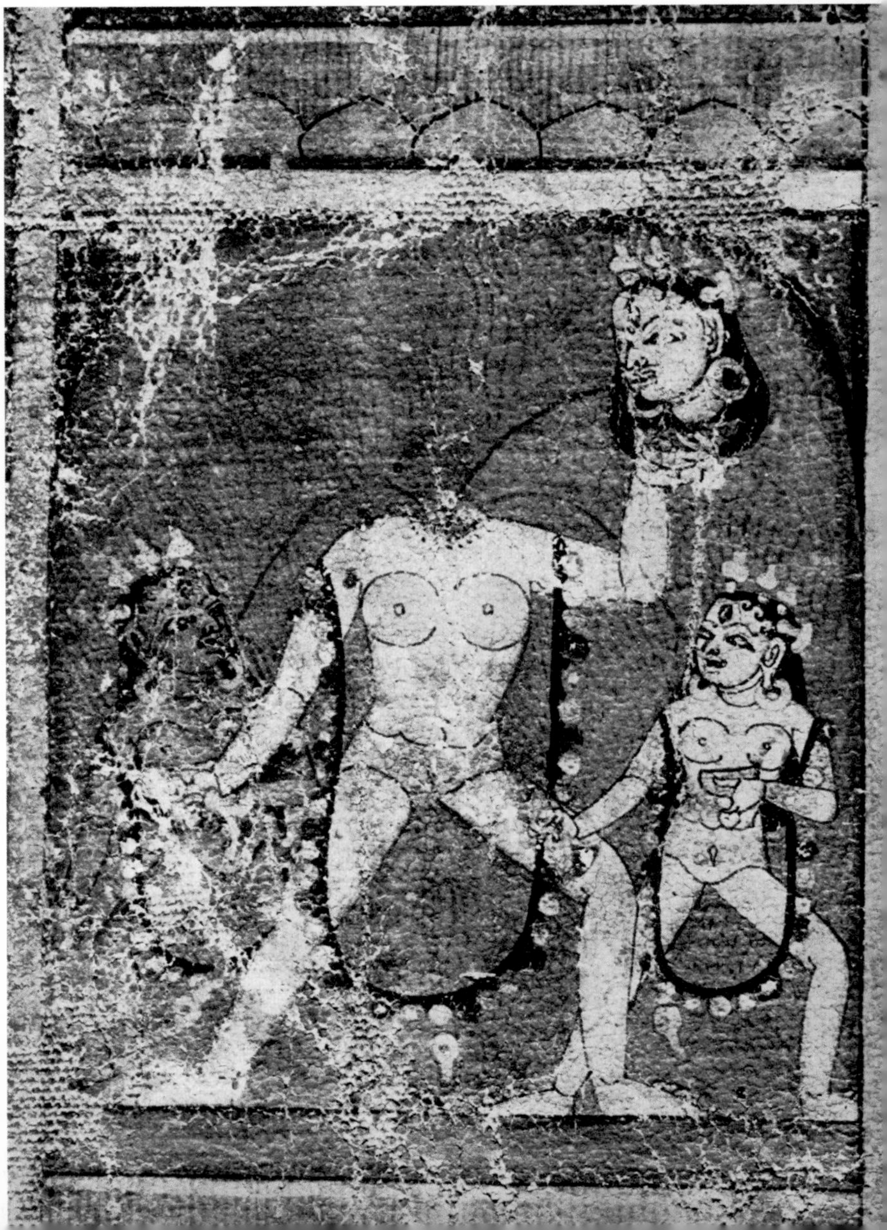

45. *Vajravārāhī; fourteenth century*
Opaque watercolor on cotton; H. 46 *in.*, W. 38 *in.*
(details above and right)

46. *Vajravārāhī; ca.* 1300
Opaque watercolor on cotton; H. 33 *in.*, W. 23½ *in. (above)*

47. *Ushṇīshavijayā; dated* 1416
Opaque watercolor on cotton; H. 28½ *in.*, W. 22½ *in. (opposite)*

48. *Kurukullā; sixteenth century*
Opaque watercolor on cotton; H. 15¾ *in.,* W. 12¾ *in. (opposite)*

49. *Dancing Female; thirteenth-fourteenth century*
Gilt copper; H. 3¼ *in. (above)*

50. *Ekajaṭā; seventeenth century*
Gilt copper; H. 12¾ *in. (right)*

51. *Ritual Crown; fifteenth century*
Gilt copper inlaid with semiprecious stones; H. 12 *in.,* W. 8½ *in. (below)*

52. *Restoration of Svayambhūnātha; dated* 1565
Opaque watercolor on cotton; H. 40½ *in.,* W. 33½ *in. (opposite)*

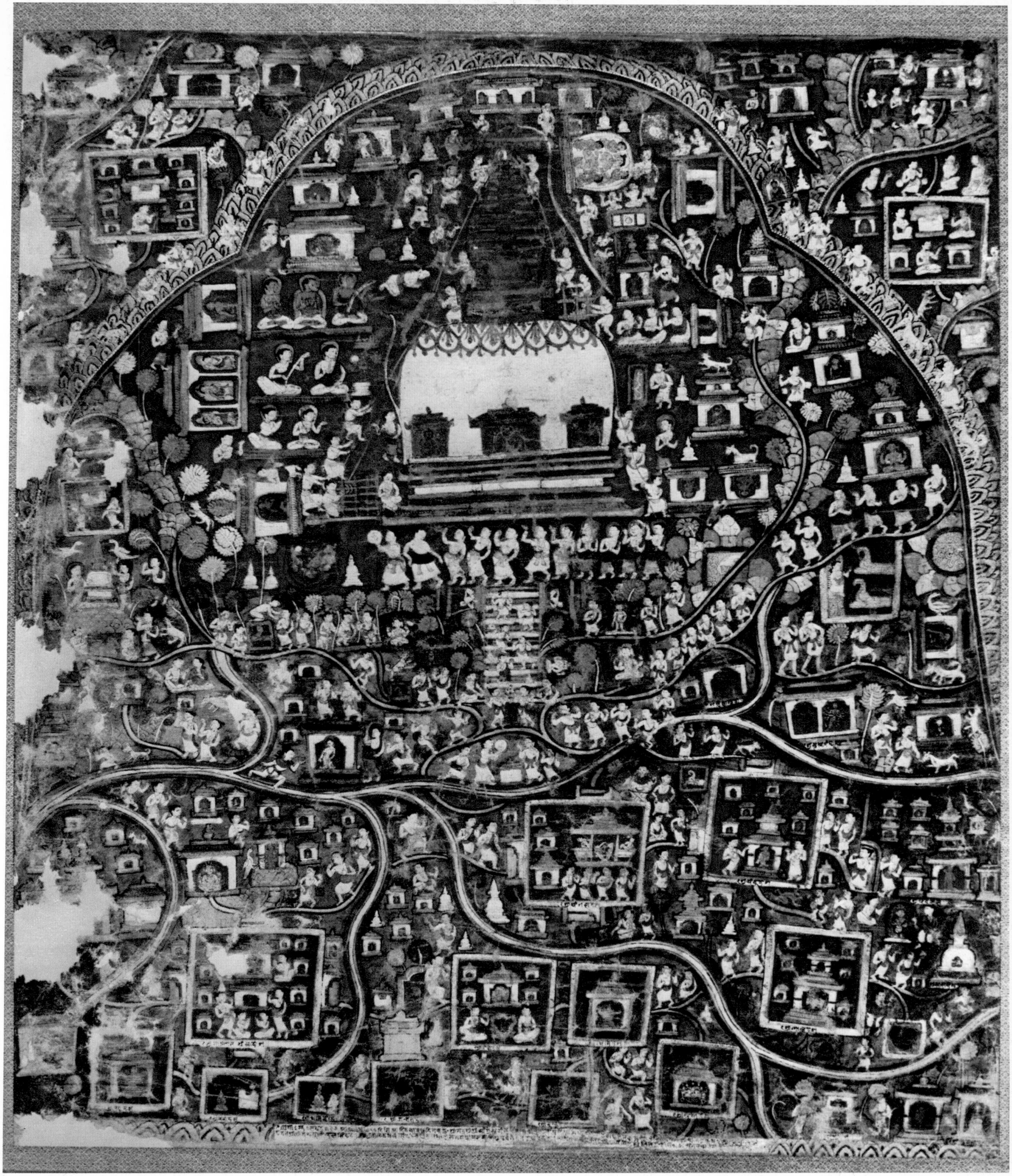

53. *A Stupa; eighteenth century*
Gilt copper repoussé; H. 23¾ *in.*, W. 10 *in.*

1. BUDDHA ŚĀKYAMUNI
Seventh century
Gilt copper; H. 19¾ *in.*
Lent by Mr. Ben Heller

The figure of the Buddha Śākyamuni stands gracefully on a shallow, rectangular base. His body is almost completely covered with a shawl, whose upper end is gathered up with a flowing sweep with his left hand. The right hand makes the gesture of munificence (*varadamudrā*). His head is covered with tiny curls and the lump on the crown (*ushṇīsha*) symbolizes his extraordinary wisdom. Other supranormal signs (*lakshaṇa*) include the elongated earlobes and the webbed fingers.

An inscription is incised on the base in the script that prevailed in Licchavi Nepal. Freely translated it reads, "For the removal of sorrow of his mother, father, and other sentient beings, this excellent image is being consecrated by the devout monk Jñānadeva." The paleography of the script, derived from Gupta India, is extremely close in style to that seen in seventh-century inscriptions. A seventh-century date seems also to be corroborated by stylistic evidence, because the figure is closely related to an almost identical Buddha still in situ in Kathmandu (cf. P. Pal, *The Arts of Nepal* [Leiden/Koln, 1974], vol. I, fig. 15).

Although the figure basically conforms to the type of Buddha image crystallized in the fifth century at Sarnath, the treatment of the garment reflects the influence of Mathura prototypes. The face has already assumed a characteristically Nepali expression, and the body reveals just such a touch of mannered elegance as one would expect in bronzes that were created after Gupta models. Noteworthy are the sensitively delineated hands with slender fingers resembling beanpods, as prescribed in manuals of Buddhist iconography.

2. BUDDHA ŚĀKYAMUNI
Ninth century
Copper alloy; H. 10½ *in.*
Lent anonymously

Iconographically, this figure of the Buddha is identical to the previous example, except that here he stands on a lotus base. Several similar Buddha images, in bronze and in stone, are known; probably all were copied from a sacrosanct model. Stylistic differences between this figure and the Heller Buddha are slight and are noticeable mainly in the treatment of the hands and of the edges and linear striations of the robe. The hands of this figure are less sensitively delineated and the webbing has almost disappeared. These differences, together with the use of the lotus as a base, lead us to attribute this bronze to a slightly later period.

The body of the Buddha displays a subtle elegance and plasticity that has an overt sensuous appeal. The outline is crisp and faultless, and a sense of movement is expressed by both the relaxed posture and the rippling edges of the garment. The classical features persist: the aquiline nose, the half-closed eyes, and the full lips.

Published: S. Czuma, "A Gupta Style Bronze Buddha," *The Bulletin of The Cleveland Museum of Art* (February 1970), p. 65; Pal, *The Arts of Nepal*, vol. I., fig. 174.

3. LIFE OF THE BUDDHA

Fourteenth century; painted in Nepal or Tibet
Opaque watercolor on cloth; H. 31½ *in.*, W. 23½ *in.*
Lent by Mr. and Mrs. Jack Zimmerman

The principal events from the life of the Buddha are illustrated in this painting. The central scene depicts the temptation of Śākyamuni by Māra, the Buddhist god of desire (see No. 4). The register immediately below Śākyamuni shows Māra and his beautiful damsels tempting Śākyamuni, and then, having failed, departing crestfallen. The other incidents portrayed are the birth, the presentation to the sage Asita, the departure, cutting of the hair, enlightenment, monkeys offering honey, the first sermon at Sarnath, the descent from the heavens, the great miracle of Śrāvastī, the taming of the mad elephant Nalagiri, and the *mahāparinirvāṇa.*

The direct stylistic relation of such paintings to earlier manuscript illuminations is evident. Several Tibetan examples, executed in a fundamentally similar manner, were first brought to light by Professor G. Tucci (see P. Pal, *The Art of Tibet* [New York: Asia House Gallery, 1969], p. 36 and no. 1), who considered them to be works rendered in a predominantly Nepali style.

4. THE TEMPTATION OF ŚĀKYAMUNI

Dated 1561
Opaque watercolor on cotton; H. 42¾ *in.*, W. 29¾ *in.*
Lent by the Museum of Fine Arts, Boston; gift of John Goelet

In his *Buddhacharita*, the poet Aśvaghosha describes Māra's attack on Śākyamuni as follows:

> "Then Mâra called to mind his own army, wishing to work the overthrow of the Śâkya saint; and his followers swarmed round, wearing different forms and carrying arrows, trees, darts, clubs, and swords in their hands; . . .
>
> Copper-red, covered with red spots, bearing clubs in their hands, with yellow or smoke-coloured hair, with wreaths dangling down, with long pendulous ears like elephants, clothed in leather or wearing no clothes at all; . . .
>
> Some as they went leaped about wildly, others danced upon one another, some sported about in the sky. . . .
>
> Such were the troops of demons who encircled the root of the Bodhi tree on every side, eager to seize it and to destroy it, awaiting command of their lord." (E. B. Cowell [tr.], *Buddhist Mahâyâna Texts* [Delhi, 1965], pt. 1, pp. 139–141).

This vivid verbal description of the attack of Māra's horde is brilliantly recreated by an unknown Nepali artist in an unusually busy painting. The artist has handled the composition with great assurance, and the calm and serene Śākyamuni in the center makes a mockery of the ferocious assault by Māra's followers. Finally, we see a despondent Māra deserting the battlefield in a chariot.

Published: P. Pal and H. C. Tseng, *Lamaist Art: The Aesthetics of Harmony* (Boston, 1969), p. 36, fig. 8.

5. BUDDHA ŚĀKYAMUNI

Sixteenth century
Gilt copper; H. 10¾ *in.*
Lent by Mr. and Mrs. Frank W. Neustatter

Seated in the classic yogic posture, the Buddha makes the gesture that symbolizes the occasion of his first sermon at Sarnath. There the Wheel of the Law was set in motion, and hence the gesture is known in Sanskrit as *dharmachakrapravartanamudrā*. That the figure represents the historical Buddha Śākyamuni rather than the transcendental Tathāgata Vairochana, who is given the same basic iconography, is evident from the peculiar design of the garment, which is covered with a pattern of rectangles outlined in high relief and intended to resemble patchwork. The tradition holds that the Buddha and other monks were in the habit of wearing garments sewn together from old clothes given to them by lay people. The texts tell us that the patchwork should resemble the rice fields of Magadha, and in fact the pattern is very like that of the segmented fields which one still sees in India and Southeast Asia today.

Except for the design of the garment, it is evident that the figure of the Buddha has not substantially changed over the centuries. However, minor stylistic changes are noticeable in the salient details as well as the facial features, which are now more frankly Nepali.

6. BUDDHA PREACHING

Dated 1649
Opaque watercolor on cloth; H. 43¼ *in.*, W. 32½ *in.*
Lent by The Cleveland Museum of Art; purchase from the J. H. Wade Fund by exchange

In the central panel of the painting, an enthroned Buddha of heroic proportions, crowned and ornamented, is engaged in preaching to the donor Jayarāma Bhāro and members of his family. Framing the Buddha are narrative scenes that appear to depict episodes from both the *Avadāna* and *Jātaka* literature. Each is identified by a brief inscription in Newari. Along the top of the painting are portrayed the Five Tathāgatas and other Buddhist deities; along the bottom are scenes of ritual dance and music and a portrait of King Pratāpamalla.

According to the dedicatory inscription at the bottom, the painting was consecrated to please the personal deity (*ishṭadevatā*) of Jayarāma Bhāro in 1649, when Pratāpamalla was reigning in Kathmandu. Jayarāma Bhāro was an influential nobleman of the period and a devout Buddhist, as is evident from this painting and other works of art that he commissioned. Obviously such a person must have employed the finest available artist. Indeed, this is one of the most beautiful paintings that has survived from seventeenth-century Nepal.

7. HEAD OF A BUDDHA IMAGE

Seventeenth century
Gilt copper with paint; H. 9⅞ *in.*, W. 8 *in.*
Lent by the Seattle Art Museum;
Eugene Fuller Memorial Collection

This impressive head must have belonged to a life-size image of the Buddha. Despite its late date, it preserves the classical Indian features with remarkable tenacity. The aquiline nose, the bow-shaped eyebrows, the half-shut eyes, shaped like lotus petals, echo features that were perfected in India almost a millennium earlier. The short, curly mass of hair is rendered in so stylized a fashion that the resultant effect is that of a wig. The abnormally elongated ear-lobes, seen also in earlier images (Nos. 1, 2), were considered a superhuman attribute. Although the tuft of hair between the eye-brows—another supernatural sign—is usually shown by a dot, during this period in Nepal, it was often rendered in the shape of an inverted question mark, as in this example.

8. BUDDHA AS THE SUPREME HEALER

Fifteenth century; painted in Tibet
Opaque watercolor on cloth; H. 20¾ *in.*, W. 17½ *in.*
Lent by Dr. Edwin Binney, 3rd

Surrounded by a host of Tathāgatas, tantric deities, apotheosized monks and guardian figures, is the enthroned figure of the Buddha as the supreme healer. Seated in the traditional yogic posture, he holds a medicine bowl in his left hand and a fruit, probably a myrobalan, in his right. Seven other isolated Buddhas at the cardinal and intermediate points complete the group of eight healing Buddhas who are peculiar to Tibetan iconography. The two Bodhisattvas immediately flanking the main figure are Sūryavairochana and Chandravairochana.

The inclusion of Tibetan monks clearly indicates that the painting was executed in Tibet. However, the majority of the figures, particularly those of the dancing goddesses below the Buddha, are unquestionably Nepali. Also derived from Nepali painting is the busy scroll motif that appears in the background and on the elaborate throne of the Buddha, which has been delineated with remarkable finesse and refinement. That the painting was done by a Nepali artist for a Tibetan patron seems an inescapable conclusion.

Published: *Thangka Art* (New York: Doris Wiener Gallery, 1974), pl. H.

9. TATHĀGATA AKSHOBHYA

Tenth–eleventh century
Copper alloy with traces of gilt; H. 8 *in.*
Lent by Mr. and Mrs. Frank W. Neustatter

The term "Tathāgata," used as a synonym for Buddha, is generally applied to transcendental rather than historical Buddhas. According to the Vajrayāna school of Buddhism, the transcendental Buddha has five principal manifestations, constituting the Pentad, from which the other members of the pantheon emanate. Akshobhya, or the Imperturbable, who is one member of the Pentad, has been given a name that originally was used to describe Buddha Śākyamuni himself. It refers to the occasion during his enlightenment at Bodhgaya, when Śākyamuni withstood the temptations of Māra, the god of desire (see Nos. 3, 4). Since there was no one else present at that time, the Buddha called upon the Earth to witness his victory over Māra. The event is symbolized by the "earth-touching" gesture that this figure makes with the right hand. Usually, the Five Tathāgatas are represented exactly as the Buddha Śākyamuni is and they can be identified only in a specific context, or by additional emblems. The emblem peculiar to Akshobhya is the *vajra* (thunderbolt), which has been portrayed on the pedestal of this bronze. It is also possible, however, that the image represents the historical Buddha in the form known as *Vajrāsana*, or "seated on the diamond throne."

The graceful figure of the Tathāgata sits in introspective calm in the classic posture of a yogi. His serenity and composure are further accentuated by contrast with the movement of the leaping tongues of flames surrounding the aureole and the nimbus. The circles of flames define the phenomenal world which a Tathāgata transcends.

Published: Pal, *The Arts of Nepal*, vol. I, fig. 184.

10. RATNASAMBHAVA AND THE EIGHT BODHISATTVAS
Twelfth century
Opaque watercolor on cotton; H. 16⅛ *in.*, W. 13 *in.*
Lent by the Los Angeles County Museum of Art; The Nasli and Alice Heeramaneck Collection

One of the earliest surviving Nepali paintings, this delicately rendered work forms a pair with another painting now in the Museum of Fine Arts, Boston (cf. J. Fontein and P. Pal, *Museum of Fine Arts, Boston: Oriental Art* [Boston, 1969], pl. 105). Since the other portrays the Tathāgata Amitābha and the central figure here is Ratnasambhava, we may assume that the two paintings belonged to a set of five, representing the Five Tathāgatas. Seated in the yogic posture, Ratnasambhava is surrounded by eight Bodhisattvas. Eight Tathāgatas appear in two panels at the top of the composition and seven other deities are arranged along the bottom. Ratnasambhava's left hand rests on his lap; his right hand makes the gesture of munificence (*varadamudrā*).

A close comparison of this painting with manuscript illuminations of the twelfth century (see No. 44) clearly establishes its date. There seems little doubt that such paintings, with their gracefully modeled figures and rich tonality of colors, are direct stylistic descendants of the Ajanta murals. In turn, Nepali paintings such as this must have strongly influenced the style of several paintings included here that may have been executed in Tibet (Nos. 3, 11, 29).

Published: P. Pal, "A Note on the Mandala of the Eight Bodhisattvas," *Archives of Asian Art*, vol. XXVI (1972–73), p. 72, fig. 4.

11. A BUDDHIST THEOPHANY
Thirteenth century; painted in Tibet or Nepal
Opaque watercolor and gold on cotton; H. 31½ *in.*, W. 25 *in.*
Lent anonymously

In the center a Tathāgata is seated on a lotus, with his left hand placed on his lap and his right displaying the gesture of reassurance (*abhayamudrā*). It is probable that the complexion of this figure is intended to be golden rather than yellow and that he represents the Buddha Śākyamuni in his transcendental aspect. He is accompanied by ten Bodhisattvas and by seven Tathāgatas, who are seated at the bottom of the painting together with a Tibetan monk, who is also provided with a halo. Two delightful *kinnaras* (mythical creatures like harpies) flank the colorful lotus on which the Buddha sits.

Despite its damaged condition, this painting remains an outstanding example of a style that seems to have developed in western Tibet in the twelfth and thirteenth centuries. That the style stems from such Nepali paintings as the Los Angeles Ratnasambhava (No. 10) is evident. However, it is very likely that other influences, especially from the schools of Bihar and Bengal, have also contributed to the creation of this remarkably strong and colorful manner. Indeed, the palette, with its brilliant yellows, greens, blues, and reds, is extraordinarily rich. Unusual also is the use of gold for the ornaments with which the figures are lavishly endowed. Despite such intense, bold colors, the painting remains a work of serene elegance.

12. DĪPAṄKARA BUDDHA
Eighteenth century
Wood and gilt copper; H. 24¼ *in. including pedestal*
Lent anonymously

Both the Hindus and the Buddhists in Nepal, as in India, consider an image naked unless it is dressed as if it were a living person. Although this figure is made substantially of wood, it is included among these bronze images to show how repoussé metal plaques were used as embellishments and also to demonstrate that the body of an image, protected by layers of clothing, is often better preserved than the face, which is constantly exposed to ritual bathing and anointment.

Dīpaṅkara is one of the Buddhas of the past, who is supposed to have lived thousands of years before Śākyamuni. His cult appears to have been more popular in China and Tibet than in India. In Nepal, the majority of his images are rather late in date and his cult may have been introduced from Tibet after the sixteenth century, when Tibet began to exercise considerable influence on Nepali Buddhism. Stylistically as well, this image reveals influences from Tibet, particularly in the manner in which the garments are delineated. The iconography of the figure is essentially the same as that of Śākyamuni.

13. A SHRINE WITH A BUDDHA IMAGE
Eighteenth century; made in Tibet
Gilt bronze inlaid with semiprecious stones; H. 35 *in.*, W. 22 *in.*
Lent anonymously

The figure within the shrine is that of Buddha Śākyamuni calling the earth to witness his victory over Māra (see Nos. 4, 9). Lions support the shrine on their backs and two serpents entwine the pilasters. Two faces of glory (*kīrttimukha*) are added as auspicious symbols at the apex of the arch and in the center of the drapery that falls between the lions at the bottom of the shrine. Immediately below the roof is a row of letters repeating the formula sacred to Lamaism: *om maṇi padme hum.*

Although the shrine is probably from Tibet, it is included here as a superb example of Newari craftsmanship. Much Tibetan metalwork was executed by Newari craftsmen or by Urhas, who were the result of intermarriage between the Newars and Tibetans. It seems likely that the Tibetans acquired a taste for gem-encrusted metalwork from the Newars, who had apparently mastered the art as early as the seventh century.

14. BODHISATTVA MAITREYA

Ninth century
Gilt copper with paint; H. 26 *in.*
Lent by the Pan-Asian Collection — *frontispiece*

This elegant and slender figure portrays Maitreya, the future Buddha, who may be represented in Buddhist art as either a Buddha or a Bodhisattva. Here Maitreya appears in the latter form and is given the jewels and ornaments typical of a Bodhisattva. His right hand displays the gesture of exposition (*vyākhyānamudrā*) appropriate to the future teacher; his left hand holds a waterpot containing the elixir of immortal life.

In terms of its grace and beauty, the figure is comparable to the finest Bodhisattvas of the Gupta period, particularly to the charming and delicately modeled figures of Sarnath. The half-shut eyes and the serene, soft expression of the face of this image effectively suggest that Maitreya, like the Bodhisattva Avalokiteśvara, is a compassionate figure. As the poet Ratnakīrti sang, "His glorious face is bright with gathered moonlight and his glance is soft with that pity that he bears within." (D. H. H. Ingalls, *An Anthology of Sanskrit Court Poetry* [Cambridge, Mass., 1965], p. 64).

Published: P. Pal, *Buddhist Art in Licchavi Nepal* (Los Angeles, 1974), fig. 71; P. Pal, "Bronzes of Nepal," *Arts of Asia*, vol. 4, no. 5 (Sept.–Oct. 1974), p. 35, fig. 7.

15. BODHISATTVA AVALOKITEŚVARA

Eleventh–twelfth century
Gilt copper; H. 23½ *in.*
Lent by Dr. Claus Virch

The Bodhisattva Avalokiteśvara is by far the most important Bodhisattva of the Mahāyāna pantheon. He is the savior *par excellence*, who will continue his efforts to guide humanity toward a state of spiritual preparedness until the arrival of the future Buddha Maitreya. Like Vishṇu, the Hindu god of preservation, Avalokiteśvara's principal attribute is the lotus (*padma*), hence he is also known as Padmapāṇi, or the Lotus-bearer. Here the god's right hand is stretched out in the gesture of munificence (*varada*) and from it is said to flow the nectar that assuages "the thirsty spirits of the dead." In the words of the poet Buddhakāra:

> May that great saint, his body formed of moonlight,
> within whose towering headdress Amitābha,
> like a rising sun encircled by dark clouds,
> furnishes a wreath of red *aśoka* blossoms,
> dispel your grief and grant you
> the streaming nectar of his peaceful happiness.
>
> (Ingalls, *An Anthology of Sanskrit Court Poetry*, p. 65).

One of the largest Nepali bronzes known, the figure is powerfully modeled, with solid limbs and torso. Its ponderous volume, however, in no way detracts from the elegance of the figure. Details such as the fingers, the design of the cloth, or the intricate crown are delicately chased, and the pleats of the *dhoti* are rendered with stylish exuberance.

16. ELEVEN-HEADED AVALOKITEŚVARA

Eleventh century; made in Nepal or Tibet
Gilt copper with traces of polychrome; H. 19⅜ *in.*
Lent by the Seattle Art Museum;
Eugene Fuller Memorial Collection

This is a more elaborate version of the form of the Bodhisattva Avalokiteśvara that we have already seen (No. 15). Because of the ten additional heads, arranged in a pyramidal formation, he is known as "Eleven-headed," or Ekādaśamukha Avalokiteśvara. The story goes that once Avalokiteśvara was so distraught with the suffering in the universe that his head split into ten pieces. His parental Tathāgata, Amitābha, picked up the pieces and put them together, adding his own head at the summit. The number ten may also refer to the eight cardinal directions plus the zenith and the nadir, or it may symbolize the ten stages of enlightenment (*daśabhūmi*), a belief held by the *Avataṁsaka* sect of Mahāyāna Buddhism.

Usually, this form of the Bodhisattva has eight arms (see No. 17) but, curiously, in this example he is given only six. Of the attributes, the lotus, the waterpot, and the wheel are easily recognized, and two of the right hands display the gestures of exposition and munificence, but the fourth emblem has not been identified.

The Eleven-headed Avalokiteśvara does not seem to have gained much popularity in India. Nepali images of the Bodhisattva are also relatively rare, and the present bronze is probably the earliest known. The lingering traces of paint indicate that this image was very likely worshipped in Tibet; in fact, it may have been made in that country by a Nepali artist.

17. ELEVEN-HEADED AVALOKITEŚVARA
Thirteenth century
Gilt copper inlaid with semiprecious stones; H. 12⅛ *in.*
Lent anonymously

Iconographically, this figure is similar to the previous example (No. 16), with the following exceptions: this Bodhisattva is provided with two additional hands, displaying the gesture of reverence (*namaskāramudrā*); the uppermost left hand of the deity holds a bow and arrow; the right hand, displaying the gesture of exposition, is here held vertically, and the wheel is provided with flames.

Stylistically, however, the two sculptures are substantially different. This elegant bronze is characterized by far stronger symmetry and decorative exuberance, manifest not only in the delineation of the *dhoti* pleats and the sash ends, but also in the treatment of the vegetal scrolls behind the feet. The two figures are further distinguished in terms of proportions as well as modeling.

18. AMOGHAPĀŚA LOKEŚVARA
Fifteenth century
Opaque watercolor on cotton; H. 24½ *in.*, W. 21 *in.*
Lent by Mr. and Mrs. Jack Zimmerman

The central figure in this painting represents Amoghapāśa Lokeśvara (one of the numerous forms of the Bodhisattva Avalokiteśvara), whose cult is especially popular among Nepali Buddhists. The Bodhisattva stands gracefully within an elaborate shrine that is typical of Buddhist paintings in Nepal. His eight hands display the rosary, the three-pronged staff (*tridaṇḍī*), gestures of exposition and munificence, the manuscript, the lotus, the noose (*pāśa*), and a pot. His four principal companions (reading counterclockwise) are the gentle Sudhanakumāra and the fierce Hayagrīva, both of whom are kneeling, the four-armed goddess Bhrikuṭī, and Tārā, the savioress. The painting also includes Buddha Śākyamuni, three Bodhisattvas, and the Five Tathāgatas. Along the bottom, rows of donors flank a priest performing the rituals of worship.

The painting can be dated quite securely because of its close stylistic correspondence with an example in Leiden dated 1436 (cf. S. Kramrisch, *The Art of Nepal* [New York: Asia House Gallery, 1964], no. 82). Indeed, so similar are they in form and color that one wonders if they are not works of the same atelier.

19. MANDALA OF AMOGHAPĀŚA LOKEŚVARA
Dated 1867
Opaque watercolor on cotton; H. 44¾ *in.*, W. 35 *in.*
Lent anonymously

The Bodhisattva Amoghapaśa Lokeśvara (see No. 18) is represented here within a mandala. Surrounding the mandala are representations of stories extolling the merits of performing a religious rite known as *ashṭamīvrata.* A different story is illustrated on each side: one concerns a King Dharmapāla, the other a King Kṛakīka. Both kings are mythical personages and the rite is very likely the same as *ashṭāṅgavrata*, performed by a king named Kṛīka during the time of Kaśyapa Buddha, as recounted in the *Avadāna-śataka.* The inscriptions on the painting not only narrate the stories, but also identify the several divinities included at the top and the bottom. The three mandalas at the top are identified as the Buddhamandala, Dharmamandala, and Samghamandala.

In terms of design and decorative motifs, the principal mandala seems to have been copied from contemporary Tibetan mandalas, and the cloud patterns and snowy mountain peaks were also inspired by Tibetan landscape motifs. After the seventeenth century, Nepali Buddhist paintings were considerably influenced by Tibetan works. In this example, however, especially in the representation of the narrative subjects, influences of the Rajput tradition are more apparent.

20. CHINTĀMAṆI LOKEŚVARA
Eighteenth century
Gilt copper with semiprecious stones; H. 7½ *in.*, W. 4¼ *in.*
Lent by Mr. and Mrs. John Gilmore Ford

In this special form, the Bodhisattva Lokeśvara or Avalokiteśvara acts essentially as a god of wealth. The word *chintāmaṇi* specifically means the "wishing gem" and, from the iconography of the representation, it is obvious that what the devotee desires is affluence. The Bodhisattva dispenses jewels as he stands in the attitude of the flute-bearing Krishṇa of the Brahmanical pantheon (see No. 84). Two gnome-like yakshas are busy collecting the gems, while two other figures with elephants' heads appear on the base. Also accompanying the Bodhisattva are two female attendants who must be manifestations of Tārā. The figures are set against an ornate and intricate foliate arch that probably symbolizes the *kalpavriksha*, or wish-fulfilling tree. The tree is richly embellished with jewels and inhabited by two monkeys. At the apex is the figure of a Tathāgata holding a bowl in his left hand and displaying the "earth-touching" gesture with his right. Usually Amitābha is considered the parental Tathāgata of the Bodhisattva, but the Tathāgata in this instance is given the gesture of Akshobhya. The bowl, however, is not an emblem of Akshobhya, and may indicate that the figure represents one of the medicine Buddhas.

This form of the Bodhisattva seems to have been created in Nepal, perhaps as late as the Malla period (thirteenth-eighteenth centuries). Most of the images that have come to light are of the sixteenth century or later. Both the iconography and the composition are strongly influenced by similar images of Krishṇa, who is sometimes portrayed standing under a *kalpavriksha* and flanked by his two wives, Rukmiṇī and Satyabhāmā.

21. A BODHISATTVA
Thirteenth century
Gilt copper inlaid with semiprecious stones; H. 19 *in.*
Lent anonymously

A graceful Bodhisattva is seated in the princely posture generally given to such regal figures as Indra (see No. 87). He is richly ornamented, and wears an elaborate crown and a necklace that are especially noteworthy. Behind the crown, his hair is beautifully coiffed into a chignon, in the manner of an Indian yogi; his ascetic nature is further indicated by the deerskin draped over his left forearm. It may be pointed out that generally the skin is flung across the left shoulder. His right hand gracefully displays the gesture of reassurance. The placement of a ring on the index finger of the left hand is unusual. Very likely, that hand once held the stem of a flower, which was attached to the left arm near the armlet. Although the crown is not adorned with an effigy of the Tathāgata Amitābha, the figure can with some certainty be identified as Avalokiteśvara.

Whatever the exact identification of the figure may be, it is an outstanding example of Nepali bronzes. Stylistically, it is a direct descendant of the earlier standing Avalokiteśvara (No. 15), and reveals the same sense of weightiness tempered by soft elegance. The ornamentation is somewhat more elaborate but, as is typical of Nepali bronzes, it does not overwhelm the form.

22. BODHISATTVA MAÑJUŚRĪ
Fifteenth century
Gilt bronze inlaid with semiprecious stones; H. 30¾ *in.*
Lent by The Cleveland Museum of Art; purchase,
Leonard C. Hanna Jr. Bequest

This imposing four-armed figure represents the Bodhisattva Mañjuśrī, seated in the lotus position, elaborately adorned with inlaid ornaments and an ornate crown similar to that worn by the preceding Bodhisattva (No. 21). His upper right hand brandishes a truncated sword and the lower right very likely held an arrow. One of his left hands holds a bow; the other makes the gesture of exposition. The stem of a blue lotus is attached to this arm, and the flower may have supported a book.

Mañjuśrī is the Buddhist god of wisdom and figures prominently in both the Mahāyāna and Vajrayāna pantheons. The book symbolizes gnosis as embodied in the *Prajñāpāramitā* text, while the flaming sword is said to destroy ignorance. Curiously Mañjuśrī, meaning "pleasing to behold," is also invariably described as a young prince, imbued with the sentiment of love. The conceptualization of the Bodhisattva seems to have been influenced by that of the god of love, Kāma, a fact that may also have determined the inclusion of the bow and arrow among his attributes.

Despite its monumentality, the bronze is a study in lyrical grace befitting the Bodhisattva's character. The unshakeable steadfastness of the posture is curiously but convincingly combined with the rhythmic curves of the torso. The sculptor obviously has achieved a great visual design, but not at the cost of a clear definition of the sculptural mass.

23. BODHISATTVA VAJRAPĀṆI
Eighth century
Copper with traces of gilt; H. 7 *in.*
Lent by the Pan-Asian Collection

This charming little bronze portrays two figures, standing gracefully on separate lotuses. The principal figure, with his elaborately coiffed hair, has his right hand raised to the chest and his left hand placed on the head of his dwarf attendant. The right hand holds a spherical object; the left lightly grasps the prongs of a thunderbolt (*vajra*) that emerges from the dwarf's crown. The dwarf has his arms folded across his chest in the gesture expressive of humility (*vinayahasta*). A snake encircles his hips.

Since the dwarf represents Vajrapurusha, the personified form of the *vajra* emblem, the principal figure may be identified as Vajrapāṇi, who figures as a constant companion and guardian of the Buddha in early Buddhist literature and art. In the Mahāyāna pantheon, Vajrapāṇi came to be regarded as a fully evolved and fairly popular Bodhisattva.

The practice of personifying the attributes of deities was common in India during the Gupta period (ca. 300–600 A.D.). It was also popular in Licchavi Nepal (ca. 400–850 A.D.) especially when representing Vajrapāṇi. Stylistically, as well as conceptually, the figure reflects the strong influence of the Gupta tradition, which made an important contribution to the art of Licchavi Nepal.

Published: Pal, *The Arts of Nepal*, vol. I, fig. 203; Pal, *Buddhist Art in Licchavi Nepal*, fig. 77; Pal, "Bronzes of Nepal," p. 34, fig. 6.

24. VAJRAPURUSHA (?)
Tenth century
Gilt copper; H. 5¼ *in.*
Lent by the Los Angeles County Museum of Art; gift of
Mr. and Mrs. Harry Kahn

This unusual bronze shows a dwarfish figure standing in a relaxed posture on a lotus base. Except for its more square shape and the addition of a beard, the face of the image is similar to that of another figure in the exhibition (No. 23). He is bedecked with snakes and sports an animal skin over his short *dhoti*. His cape spreads out behind him in a fan shape, almost creating the illusion of wings, and his arms are crossed against his chest in the gesture known as *vinayahasta*. Emerging from his head are the four prongs of what appears to be an open thunderbolt (*vajra*).

Because of this *vajra*-like protrusion, the author suggests that the figure be identified as Vajrapurusha (see No. 23). Although the presence of the serpents and the wing-like cape may lead some to consider him to be a Garuḍa, the gesture, to the author's knowledge, is never associated with Garuḍa. On the other hand, in Nepal there is a consistent tradition of portraying Vajrapurusha with his arms similarly disposed.

25. BODHISATTVA VAJRAPĀṆI
Ninth–tenth century
Gilt copper; H. 8 *in.*
Lent by Mr. and Mrs. Jack Zimmerman

A rather ferocious figure is portrayed dancing on a corpse placed upon a lotus. The figure is clad in a *dhoti* over which is draped an animal skin, probably that of a tiger. His ornaments and sacred cord take the form of snakes, which accentuate his forbidding appearance. His angry expression is further emphasized by his matted hair, round staring eyes, and open mouth displaying fangs. His left hand is raised in the gesture of admonition (*tarjanīmudrā*); the right hand holds a thunderbolt.

Very likely the figure represents one of the angry manifestations of the Bodhisattva Vajrapāṇi (see No. 23). Such terrifying forms of Vajrapāṇi are of considerable importance in the tantric Buddhist pantheon for he is generally regarded as one of the principal defenders of the faith. As is evident from details such as the third eye and the snake ornaments, this figure has been strongly influenced by Bhairava, the angry form of Śiva (No. 63). Moreover, in this rather unusual representation, Vajrapāṇi is shown dancing, an activity traditionally associated with Śiva.

26. BODHISATTVA VAJRAPĀṆI
Twelfth century
Gilt bronze; H. 10 *in.*
Lent by Mr. Paul F. Walter

This bronze portrays the more conventional form of Vajrapāṇi in his angry manifestation. Although he is the same Bodhisattva that we have encountered in the Zimmerman image (No. 25), the differences between the two figures are pronounced. Here Vajrapāṇi stands with both feet firmly placed upon the lotus base in the posture generally known as *pratyālīḍha*. The serpent ornaments are altogether dispensed with, as is the corpse, and on the figure's head is placed a small effigy of the Tathāgata Akshobhya. In contrast to the expression on the face of the Zimmerman bronze, the demeanor here seems almost placid. Perhaps the most significant differences between the two figures are apparent in their postures and in the proportions of their bodies. The Zimmerman Vajrapāṇi has a relatively slim, athletic body, while this figure is characterized by the corpulence that is more commonly seen in such images of angry deities.

Published: P. Pal, "Indian Art from the Paul Walter Collection," *Allen Memorial Art Museum Bulletin*, vol. XXVIII, no. 2 (1971), pp. 100–101.

27. MAHĀCHAKRA VAJRAPĀṆI
Fifteenth century
Gilt bronze with polychrome, inlaid with semiprecious stones; H. 13¼ *in.*
Lent by Mr. and Mrs. John Gilmore Ford

In this tantric form, Vajrapāṇi is known as Mahāchakra and is generally portrayed in coitus with his female partner. Below their feet are two outstretched figures who may represent Hindu deities. The left leg of the female is thrown vigorously around the god's waist. Her left arm encircles his neck and her left hand holds a skull; her right hand brandishes the chopper. Vajrapāṇi's principal hands are crossed in the gesture known as *vajrahuṁkāra*. His two upper hands display the thunderbolt and the gesture of admonition; the two lower hands let loose the snakes that are shown triumphing over the prostrate figures. The deities are profusely ornamented and Vajrapāṇi is given an animal skin as a garment. Both are provided with a third eye, showing once again the influence of Śaiva iconography on Buddhist images.

Although the manifestation is ostensibly an angry one, the god's face glows with the sentiment of love. The sculptor has beautifully balanced the two figures who appear completely absorbed in one another. As if following the invisible perimeter of a mandala, the flowing, circular outline is emphatically articulated not only by the disposition of Vajrapāṇi's arms, but also by the billowing scarf and the snakes. The details of garments and jewelry are rendered with great finesse and it is quite remarkable that so complex a concept has been given such an easily comprehensible and visually appealing form.

Published: P. Pal, *Indo-Asian Art from the John Gilmore Ford Collection* (Baltimore, 1971), p. 45, fig. 57; Pal, *The Arts of Nepal*, vol. I, fig. 282.

28. TWO EMBRACING TANTRIC DEITIES
Fifteenth century
Silver with polychrome; H. 5 *in.*
Lent by Doris Wiener

Although tantric Buddhist deities are frequently represented in sexual embrace, this delightful silver image is unusual in that the female seems to be the principal figure; the male is distinctly the smaller of the two. The female's arms encircle the male and her hands are crossed in the *vajrahuṁkāramudrā* as they grasp a chopper and a skull-cup. The god's hands display a double thunderbolt and a bell with a double thunderbolt handle. Whether this change in the usual proportional relationship of the couple reflects an unknown theological precept or an idiosyncratic misunderstanding on the part of the artist is difficult to determine.

Their torsos are completely naked, but both figures wear identical garments wrapped around their waists. They are crowned and adorned with jewelry, and the floral designs on the garments are chased with a jeweller's precision. The soles of their feet are marked with lines and decorated with a floral symbol, perhaps the lotus, thereby clearly announcing their divine character.

The sculpture is a superb realization, in artistic form, of the Buddhist concept of nonduality, which is the very essence of Ultimate Reality. The figures seem to melt into one another as they embrace in a fashion that is uncommon for such images. Although they represent gods, the delineation is essentially human and naturalistic. This naturalism is achieved not only by the sensitive modeling of their bodies, but also by the expressions on their faces. The lips are about to touch and the eyes are already engaged.

29. VAJRASATTVA AND CONSORT
Fourteenth century; painted in Nepal or Tibet
Opaque watercolor on cotton; H. 14½ *in.*, W. 13 *in.*
Lent by Mr. and Mrs. Jack Zimmerman

The central couple, elaborately bejeweled, represents the Bodhisattva Vajrasattva and his female consort, Vajrasattvātmikā. Although he is a popular deity of tantric Buddhism, his exact position in the pantheon is not clearly determined. In Nepal, he has generally been regarded as the priest of the Five Tathāgatas. In this representation the Bodhisattva holds his two attributes, the *vajra* and the bell. His companion has her right arm around his shoulders and holds a bell with her left hand, which is unusual, as she is supposed to hold a chopper and a skull-cup. While it is not possible here to identify all the subsidiary deities surrounding Vajrasattva, mention may be made of the three forms of Kubera, the god of wealth, included in the lower left hand corner.

That the painting was intended for Tibetan patrons is clear from the representations of the king and queen as well as the general among the "seven jewels," the emblems and counselors of a Universal Monarch, in the lowermost register. Their attire is unquestionably Tibetan. At the same time, if we compare the painting with that of Amoghapāśa Lokeśvara (No. 18), it is evident that the style is predominantly Nepali. It is difficult to determine, however, whether the painting was executed in Nepal for a Tibetan patron or painted by a Nepali artist in Tibet.

Whatever its provenance, the painting is a delightful work of art. Especially appealing is the charming portrayal of intimacy between Vajrasattva and his consort. Despite the hieratic nature of the work, the couple is shown subsumed by the sentiment of love. Equally noteworthy is the artist's sense of whimsy, evident in the comic representation of the animals, especially the rampant griffins flanking the central couple and the grinning faces below the lotus throne.

30. A LOTUS MANDALA
Eleventh–twelfth century
Copper alloy cast in several pieces; H. *(closed)* 6¼ *in.*, W. *(open)* 6½ *in.*
Lent by Mr. and Mrs. Jack Zimmerman

It will be apparent from several paintings in the exhibition (Nos. 19, 43, 80) that the center of a mandala is almost invariably a lotus. This extraordinary object, with its movable petals, represents a lotus mandala in three dimensions. In the center of the mandala stands the esoteric Buddhist deity Hevajra in union with his consort. As the Lord himself declares in the *Hevajra-tantra* "There at its centre am I, O Fair One, together with you. The Joy Innate I am in essence, and impassioned with great passion." (D. Snellgrove, *The Hevajra Tantra* [London, 1959], pt. 1, p. 110.) As the two embrace in the center of the mandala, from their union emerge, successively, eight goddesses: Gaurī, Chaurī, Vetālī, Ghasmarī, Pukkasī, Śavarī, Chaṇḍālī and Ḍombinī. The goddesses are dancing for it is their ultimate function to arouse Hevajra, who "sinks with his spell into the condition of bliss." (*ibid.*).

31. HEVAJRA
Twelfth–thirteenth century
Copper with traces of gilt; H. 9¾ *in.*
Lent anonymously

Here Hevajra is represented alone in a dancing posture. His right foot tramples an outstretched figure who appears to be looking up at the god with some curiosity; his left leg is folded and turned towards the right thigh. One of the right arms is bent across his body in a rather unusual fashion; the remaining fifteen arms are spread out fan-like on either side. Each hand holds a skull-cup and in each cup are animals or humans. According to textual sources, the skulls in the right hands should contain an elephant, a horse, an ass, an ox, a camel, a man, a lion, and a cat. Those in the left should hold earth, water, fire, air, sun, moon, Yama, and Vaiśravaṇa (Snellgrove, *The Hevajra Tantra*, pt. 1, p. 111). The deity is given five heads, the four principal heads being marked with the vertical third eye, which is an iconographic detail obviously borrowed from Śiva.

An important god of tantric Buddhism, Hevajra is the central figure of a cult that has been particularly popular in both Nepal and Tibet. Although the cult is an esoteric one, it seems to have appealed especially to the Mahāsiddhas, devotees who achieved seemingly super-human powers through the use of mental exercises and played a significant role in popularizing Vajrayāna Buddhism. From the attributes held by the god, it is evident that he was regarded as a sort of Universal Being like the Viśvarūpa form of Vishṇu.

32. SAMBARA WITH CONSORT
Ca. 1500
Opaque watercolor on cotton; H. 54 *in.*, W. 45 *in.*
Los Angeles County Museum of Art; formerly The Nasli and Alice Heeramaneck Collection, Museum Associates' Purchase

Sambara, who is regarded as a manifestation of Hevajra (Nos. 30, 31), is one of the most important deities of Vajrayāna Buddhism. The form illustrated here corresponds exactly to the description given in the *Nishpannayogāvalī*, an important tantric text of the eleventh century (see Bhattacharyya, *The Indian Buddhist Iconography*, p. 162). Sambara is shown in coition with his consort, Vajravārāhī (see Nos. 45, 46). Their embrace symbolizes the union between wisdom and method which leads to ultimate bliss. The deities are portrayed against a background of flaming red which defines the fiery field of wisdom and which is surrounded by the eight cemeteries symbolizing the phenomenal world. Wrathful deities are represented both above and below the central pair, and the majority of them are also engaged in copulation with their female partners.

In both the harmony of its composition and the intricacy of its details, this painting is a *tour de force*. "Calm is the innate," says the text, and so indeed are the representations of the principal *dramatis personae*. Viewed in segments, the painting is characterized by intense activity in each area. Vajravārāhī's passionate embrace is amplified by the strong tonality of the dancing flames of the aureole and the intense blue, highlighted by grays, of Sambara. Viewed as a whole, however, the painting becomes a symbol of tranquility in which the transcendental reality, symbolized by Sambara and Vajravārāhī, is harmonized with phenomenal experience, represented by the surrounding cemeteries with their corpses and fires, goblins and animals.

33. CHAṆḌAMAHĀROSHAṆA
Sixteenth century
Opaque watercolor on cotton; H. 34 *in.*, W. 26 *in.*
Lent by Mr. and Mrs. Jack Zimmerman

The importance of this deity in tantric Buddhism is evident from the fact that an entire *tantra* known as the *Chaṇḍamahāroshaṇa-tantra* was devoted to him. His cult, however, was an extremely esoteric one, and his images were shown only to the initiates. Chaṇḍamahāroshaṇa is also known by the epithet, Achala, which means "immovable." He may be the same as another Achala who is one of the directional guardians and is often included in mandalas.

Blue in complexion, Chaṇḍamahāroshaṇa is represented here against a sea of flames. He is in a semi-kneeling posture, engaged in coition with his consort, or *prajña*. His right hand brandishes a sword, and his left hand holds a noose while displaying the gesture of admonition (*tarjanīmudrā*). The noose is used to catch evil-doers; the sword cuts through the fog of ignorance. His female companion holds a skull-cup with her left hand and embraces her partner with her right. Eight other effigies of Chaṇḍamahāroshaṇa are portrayed in the flaming aureole; the remaining field of the *paubhā* is filled with other esoteric deities, Mahāsiddhas (see No. 31), monks, and scenes of ritual initiation.

34. CHAṆḌAMAHĀROSHAṆA
Seventeenth century
Opaque watercolor on cotton; H. 32¼ *in.*, W. 23 *in.*
Lent by Mr. and Mrs. John Gilmore Ford

Despite the fact that the *paubhās* were often based on the same iconographic tradition, two paintings portraying the same theme can differ radically. If we compare this painting of Chaṇḍamahāroshaṇa with that in the Zimmerman Collection (No. 33), not only do we find iconographic differences, such as the exclusion here of the Mahāsiddhas and the inclusion of four instead of eight Achala figures, but the variations in stylistic details, particularly in treatment of the figures, are also quite palpable. Obviously such distinctions must reflect the individual preferences of the artists.

35. AN ANGRY GOD
Tenth-eleventh century
Gilt copper with gold paint; H. 15 *in.*
Lent by the Pan-Asian Collection

Although the exact identification of this figure remains a mystery, he probably belongs to the Buddhist pantheon. At one time his right hand may have carried a sword of which only the hilt remains; his left hand displays the gesture of admonition (*tarjanī-mudrā*), which is in keeping with his angry mien. His glaring eyes, knotted eyebrows, and bared teeth graphically express his anger. His posture, too, announces his militancy. Around his neck is a necklace consisting of gems, charms, and tiger claws (*vyāghranakha*). Generally, such a necklace is worn either by Mañjuśrī of the Buddhist pantheon or Kumāra of the Brahmanical pantheon. Very likely, therefore, the figure represents an angry form of Mañjuśrī, whose principal attribute is usually a sword. Alternatively, it may represent an unusual variation of Achala Chaṇḍamahāroshaṇa, who also brandishes a sword (Nos. 33, 34).

Traces of blue pigment still decorate the hair, and the face of this figure is painted in gold, indicating that the bronze must have been worshipped in Tibet. However, the stylistic evidence overwhelmingly indicates a Nepali origin for the statue. In all probability, it was carried into Tibet by a pilgrim returning from Nepal.

36. TĀRĀ

Seventh century
Copper alloy; H. 11⅞ *in.*
Lent by Dr. Samuel Eilenberg

The goddess Tārā epitomizes the influence of the much older Mother-goddess cults upon the Mahāyāna religion. Her concept evolved in India and, by the Gupta period, she had become the most important goddess in the Mahāyāna pantheon. She was conceived primarily as a savioress and is, therefore, the female counterpart of the Bodhisattva Avalokiteśvara. She is also generally regarded as his consort and is frequently portrayed with him.

Her most distinctive emblem is the lotus which she carries in her left hand. It should be pointed out, however, that since the lotus is a ubiquitous symbol of beauty and elegance in Indian and Nepali art, it is an appropriate emblem for any goddess. In the Brahmanical pantheon, the lotus is specifically associated with both Vishṇu and his consort, Śrī-Lakshmī. In the Buddhist pantheon, it is the primary symbol of Avalokiteśvara. In addition to the lotus, the goddess here holds a spherical object, or boss, with her right hand, which is stretched out in the gesture of munificence (*varada-mudrā*). In the context of Tārā's role as a fertility deity, this boss must be regarded as a fertility symbol. In Nepal, however, a similar object is frequently held by other female figures.

The hieratically frontal posture of the figure enhances both her dignity and monumentality, the flowing ends of the garments convey a sense of movement, and the mellifluous contours of her body infuse her ample form with quiet grace. The date for this figure is suggested by a comparison with several other images which usually have been considered to be of the seventh or eighth century (cf. Kramrisch, *The Art Nepal*, nos. 2, 4; Pal, *The Arts of Nepal*, vol. I, fig. 216).

37. TĀRĀ

Eleventh century
Gilt copper; H. 8$\frac{5}{16}$ *in.*
Lent anonymously

The goddess stands gracefully on a lotus base, the outward thrust of her right hip balanced by the swinging end of her drapery. Her head is set off by a nimbus embellished with a design of flames and pearls. The face has been worn away by ritual unguents that must have been rubbed over it repeatedly for centuries; the lotus once held in the figure's hand is missing.

That she is a direct stylistic descendant of the Eilenberg Tārā (No. 36) is evident. The form, however, is more slender, and there is now a stronger emphasis on linear definition. It is remarkable how closely this bronze resembles another image of Tārā now in the British Museum (see D. Barrett, "The Buddhist Art of Tibet and Nepal," *Oriental Art*, n.s. vol. III, no. 3 [Summer 1957], p. 93, fig. 8). Indeed, were it not for the fact that the present bronze is three inches shorter, the two might have been regarded as a pair. There seems little doubt that the two images are works of the same atelier.

38. TĀRĀ

Fourteenth century
Gilt copper with semiprecious stones and paint; H. 20¼ *in.*
Lent by The Metropolitan Museum of Art; Louis V. Bell Fund

Unlike the earlier Tārā (No. 37), this image of the goddess makes the gesture of exposition with her left hand and has a lotus attached to her arm. The modeling here is less subtle and the ornamentation has increased considerably. Especially noteworthy are the elaborate crown, the ribbons flying from behind the ears, and the strands of pearls that artfully and sensuously accentuate the breasts. In terms of proportions the figure here is considerably more elongated, and the facial features are now more blatantly Mongoloid. The manner of attaching the lotus stalk to the left arm appears to have been a characteristic developed in Nepal sometime after the twelfth century. The fact that the face has been painted with gold indicates that the bronze was once worshipped in Tibet.

Published: Fong Chow, "Arts from the Rooftop of Asia—Tibet, Nepal, Kashmir," *The Metropolitan Museum of Art Bulletin*, n.s. vol. 29, no. 9 (May, 1971), p. 380; Pal, *The Arts of Nepal*, vol. I, fig. 230.

39. MAHĀŚRĪ TĀRĀ WITH COMPANIONS

Tenth century
Gilt copper; H. 8 *in.*
Lent by the Los Angeles County Museum of Art;
The Nasli and Alice Heeramaneck Collection

The central goddess, seated on a lotus and displaying the gesture of turning the Wheel of the Law (*dharmachakrapravartanamudrā*) with her hands, is Mahāśrī Tārā. She is a special form of the Tārā we have already encountered (Nos. 36–38). In this manifestation, however, she does not hold a lotus in her hand.

She is accompanied by two of her four traditional companions, who stand beside her on separate lotuses. The figure on her left is Ekajaṭā, who salutes her mistress with her right hand; the figure on her right represents Aśokakāntā, who holds the thunderbolt in her right hand and a vase in her left.

All three of the lotuses on which the deities rest rise from the same stem, which is engulfed by lush foliage that is richly and stylishly delineated, in contrast to the elegantly simple figures. Despite its rather modest scale, the bronze is a charming example of harmonious visual design and graceful modeling. The figure of Tārā, with its soft and sensuous form, is especially appealing.

Published: *The Arts of India and Nepal: The Nasli and Alice Heeramaneck Collection* (Boston, 1966), p. 80, no. 82.

40. GREEN TĀRĀ

Ca. 1300
Opaque watercolor on cotton; H. 20½ *in.*, W. 17 *in.*
Lent by The Cleveland Museum of Art;
the J. H. Wade Fund, by exchange

The goddess, enthroned within an elaborate shrine, is Tārā in her green form. With her right hand she blesses a seated monk; her left hand holds a blue lotus. An additional blue lotus is attached to her right arm.

The shrine, crowned by three stupas, is of the variety more commonly seen in eastern Indian manuscript illuminations. Unusual, however, is the cluster of trees that surrounds the tiered roofs of the shrine, clearly indicating its location in a wooded grove. Symbolically, this serves to corroborate the Mother-goddess aspect of Tārā's cult for the mother goddesses were and still are worshipped in such groves. The blue background of the painting is strewn with flowers to signify the divine presence.

While the brilliant hues reflect the artist's superb feeling for color, the composition reveals his extraordinary sense of design. The details, whether of architecture or foliage, are rendered with unusual delicacy, and yet the work is not constrained by fastidiousness. The drawing is effortless, and the entire composition sparkles with spontaneity and gemlike brilliance.

41. VASUDHĀRĀ

Dated 1082
Gilt copper inlaid with semiprecious stones; H. 8½ *in.*
Lent by Mr. and Mrs. Douglas J. Bennet, Jr.

Vasudhārā is the Buddhist goddess of wealth and is, therefore, the counterpart of the Brahmanical goddess of wealth, Śrī-Lakshmī. Vasudhārā's cult has remained extremely popular with Nepali Buddhists and, judging by her innumerable images, it is evident that she is a household deity. In this bronze we see her with six arms, a form that is ubiquitous in Nepal. With her six hands she displays the gestures of munificence and adoration of the Buddha, a cluster of jewels, a water pot, a sheaf of corn, and a manuscript. Thus both her fertility and naiad-like aspects are emphasized by her emblems. In addition, the manuscript stresses her gnostic quality.

One of the few Nepali bronzes of any antiquity inscribed with a date, this example is of particular historical significance. In addition, the sculpture differs from all other known images of Vasudhārā because of the four Tathāgatas represented in her crown. The Tathāgata in front is Vairochana while Amitābha is at the back. The two Tathāgatas on the sides are Ratnasambhava and Amoghasiddhi. Obviously the thunderbolt emerging from the crown represents the fifth Tathāgata, Akshobhya (see No. 9). Vasudhārā's association with all Five Tathāgatas clearly indicates her universal significance.

42. VASUDHĀRĀ

Twelfth century
Bronze inlaid with semiprecious stones; H. 19 *in.*
Lent by the Los Angeles County Museum of Art;
The Nasli and Alice Heeramaneck Collection

Iconographically almost identical to the eleventh-century bronze (No. 41), this figure is noticeably different stylistically. Not only are her proportions more attractive, but her form is more elegant. Especially charming is the face with its softly modeled, expressive features. Although her figure is the embodiment of physical desirability, Vasudhārā emanates an extraordinary sense of equipoise and serenity that envelops her in an aura of spiritual grace. The additional arms are so skillfully disposed that the outline seems to circumscribe an invisible aureole in the form of a mandala.

Published: *The Arts of India and Nepal: Heeramaneck Collection*, p. 85, no. 90.

43. MANDALA OF VASUDHĀRĀ

Dated 1367

Opaque watercolor on cotton; H. 40¾ *in.*, W. 34½ *in.*

Lent anonymously

The Buddhist goddess of wealth is portrayed here at the center of a mandala. (For a detailed discussion of the mandala and the relevant textual materials, see P. Pal, *Two Buddhist Paintings from Nepal* [Amsterdam, 1967].) In three registers, one at each side, and one immediately above the central mandala, are represented what appear to be episodes from the story of *Suchandra avadāna*. The story emphasizes the importance of worshipping the goddess, using the example of a certain Suchandra, a non-believer who was converted by Vasudhārā. Rather unusual is the inclusion of the eight great miracles from the life of the Buddha, depicted along the upper of the two registers at the bottom of the painting. The lowermost register illustrates scenes of dedication, ritual initiation, and festive music and dance.

This mandala is significant not only because it is the earliest dated *paubhā* that has so far come to light, but also because of its exceptional quality. Although the mandala, with its intricate gateways, flame-ringed multicolored lotus petals, and cusped arches enclosing various divinities, dominates the visual design, the narrative panels with their succinct, lively portrayals of myths and miracles are equally engrossing. Perhaps the most striking element, however, is the remarkably successful use of the intense Nepali red that seems to burst before our eyes like a lush spray of poinsettias.

Published: *Thangka Art*, pl. T.; *Art News*, vol. 73, no. 3 (March 1974), p. 97.

44. TWO COVERS AND FIVE FOLIOS OF A PAÑCHARAKSHĀ MANUSCRIPT

Dated 1138

Ink and color on wood and palm leaves; Covers: H. 2½ *in.*, W. 22½ *in. Leaves:* H. 2¼ *in.*, W. 21⅞ *in.*

Lent by Dr. Edwin Binney, 3rd

The illuminations on the five leaves portray the following goddesses (reading from top to bottom); Mahāmantrānuśāriṇī, Mahāsāhasrapramardanī, Mahāśītavatī, Mahāmāyūrī and Mahāpratisarā. Collectively these five goddesses constitute what is known as the Pañcharakshā, literally meaning "five protections." Each personifies one of the prophylactic spells, or *dhāranī*, that form the text of the manuscript. Although each has multiple heads and arms, only one of them, Mahāsāhasrapramardanī, is represented as an angry deity. Like the Bible, the *Pañcharakshā*, which is probably the most venerated Vajrayāna text, was copied and illuminated endlessly. The cover illustrated at the top shows the goddess Prajñāpāramitā flanked by six Pāramitās (see also detail). On the other cover are represented the Five Tathāgatas and two Bodhisattvas. Lively figures of monks and donors appear at the ends of each cover.

A comparison with a nearly contemporary *paubhā* (No. 10) shows that at this time there was no fundamental stylistic difference between the illuminated manuscripts and the larger paintings. In spite of their tiny scale, the illuminations reflect the same attention to detail and penchant for rich masses of color as the larger works.

45. VAJRAVĀRĀHĪ

Fourteenth century

Opaque watercolor on cotton; H. 46 *in.*, W. 38 *in.*

Lent anonymously

Although quite damaged, this exceptionally large painting is included here because of its extraordinary quality and its historical importance. In the center of the painting is portrayed the Buddhist goddess Vajravārāhī dancing exuberantly, with one leg resting on a prostrate male and the other raised and bent. Decorated with skull garlands, fluttering scarves, and bells, she brandishes a chopper with her right hand and a skull-cup with her left. A sow's head protrudes from the right side of her head and a staff is balanced under her left arm. Apart from ornamental embellishments she is completely naked, and the muted red of her complexion contrasts dramatically with the richer red of the aureole with its leaping tongues of flame.

Vajravārāhī is very likely a Buddhist counterpart of the Brahmanical goddess Vārāhī (No. 70). This seems to be substantiated by the fact that many of the goddesses included in the marginal registers are actually forms of another Brahmanical deity, Durgā, who is Śiva's consort. In fact, in Nepal Vajravārāhī is especially venerated as Vajrayoginī and seldom distinguished from Durgā.

Although executed slightly later than the Tibetan painting of Vajravārāhī included here (No. 46), the close stylistic relationship between the two works need hardly be stressed. The style of the figures represented in the little vignettes is still strongly reminiscent of the earlier palm leaf illustrations, and it seems likely that this painting was contemporaneous with the Vasudhārā mandala of 1367 A.D. (No. 43).

46. VAJRAVĀRĀHĪ

Ca. 1300; *painted in Tibet*

Opaque watercolor on cotton; H. 33 *in.*, W. 23½ *in.*

Lent anonymously

The central figure of dancing Vajravārāhī (see No. 45) and those of her six companions are set off against a rectangular panel of intense red, conspicuously isolated from the rest of the painting. This panel is surrounded by eight cemeteries, each separated from the other by strips of water representing rivers. At the top and bottom of the composition are rows of Tibetan monks and deities.

The cemeteries are rendered as vignettes, filled with Bodhisattvas, Dikpālas (guardians), attendants, serpent-kings, scavenging birds and beasts, dead bodies, fires, and stupas. Like the central composition and the figure of Vajravārāhī, the cemeteries are typically Nepali in terms of both their conceptualization and delineation. The figures in the cemeteries as well as the deities in the upper and lower registers are rendered in the same basic style as that seen in two other paintings (Nos. 3, 11). Thus, although the painting was probably executed in Tibet, once again we encounter a strong stylistic dependence on the Nepali aesthetic tradition.

47. USHṆĪSHAVIJAYĀ

Dated 1416
Opaque watercolor on cotton; H. 28½ *in.*, W. 22½ *in.*
Lent by Mr. and Mrs. Jack Zimmerman

The goddess represented within the stupa is Ushṇīshavijayā. Like the Pañcharakshā goddesses (No. 44), she is the personification of a *dhāraṇī* (spell), but the reason for her depiction within the womb of a stupa, or chaitya, is not clear. She is seated between a red and a green Bodhisattva. Interspersed between the rows of chaityas that surround the central composition are the eight guardians and, at the corners, four forms of Tārā are represented within chaityas. Five Tathāgatas, flanked by two Bodhisattvas and the sun and the moon gods, appear in the top register. The upper of the two registers at the bottom shows the Pañcharakshā deities with Achala and Vajrapāṇi at either end; the lower register illustrates scenes of ritual consecration.

According to the inscription, the painting was consecrated by one Jasarāja. The religious ceremony held on the occasion of the consecration is known as *lakshachaitya*, a term meaning that the donor vows to establish a hundred thousand (*laksha*) chaityas. With its multiple chaityas, the painting in effect symbolizes such a donation. Among the large number of paintings of *lakshachaitya* that have survived, this example is not only one of the earliest, but also probably the most attractive. The integration of the chaityas and the several compartments creates a most pleasing visual design.

48. KURUKULLĀ

Sixteenth century; painted in Tibet
Opaque watercolor on cotton; H. 15¾ *in.*, W. 12¾ *in.*
Lent by the Museum of Fine Arts, Boston; gift of John Goelet

Kurukullā is regarded by the Buddhists as their goddess of love. She is, therefore, the Buddhist counterpart of the Hindu god of desire, Kāmadeva, and like him, is engaged in shooting arrows of desire. Her other emblems are a blue lotus and an elephant-goad. Although she is the love goddess, she is generally portrayed as an awesome figure. The third eye, the slightly visible fangs, the garland of severed heads, and the tiger skin, as well as her aggressive posture, are hardly conducive to inflaming the sentiment of love. That she is here regarded as an emanation of the goddess Tārā (Nos. 36–40) is evident from the inclusion of the latter at the top of the painting. Tārā is flanked by two Tibetan monks.

The presence of the monks and the blue-green mountains clearly indicates that the painting was commissioned, and very likely executed, in Tibet. However, a comparison with the contemporary Nepali painting of Sambara (No. 32) makes the stylistic relationship of the two works abundantly clear. That the artist responsible for the Kurukullā painting was a Nepali working in Tibet seems a reasonable assumption.

Published: Pal and Tseng, *Lamaist Art*, pp. 46–47, no. 33.

49. DANCING FEMALE

Thirteenth–fourteenth century
Gilt copper; H. 3¼ *in.*
Lent by Mrs. George H. Bunting

Very likely this female figure represents one of the subsidiary Buddhist goddesses such as Nrityā, the personification of the dance, but her exact identification is difficult to determine. Although the goddess's form is idealized, only from life could the artist have realized such naturalistic imagery, and it is evident that the sculptor was thoroughly familiar with the movement and language of the dance.

50. EKAJAṬĀ

Seventeenth century
Gilt copper; H. 12¾ *in.*
Lent by the Asian Art Museum of San Francisco;
The Avery Brundage Collection

The name Ekajaṭā literally means "one whose hair is arranged in a single chignon." It is evident from the hair style of this image that the artist has faithfully followed this precept. Ekajaṭā is generally portrayed as a ferocious goddess. Her awesomeness is emphasized here by her glaring eyes and strongly marked eyebrows, her rotund belly circumscribed by a snake, and her emblems, the chopper and the skull-cup. The lotus attached to her upper left arm announces her affiliation with the goddess Tārā (see No. 36). It is claimed that her cult originated in Tibet.

The continued vitality of the Nepali aesthetic tradition is evident in such repoussé work. The artist is still attentive to details and the floral designs are especially elegant.

Published: Pal, *The Arts of Nepal,* vol. I, fig. 243.

51. RITUAL CROWN

Fifteenth century
Gilt copper inlaid with semiprecious stones; H. 12 *in.,* W. 8½ *in.*
Lent anonymously

Although such crowns are often seen in Nepali paintings, worn either by the gods or by the Buddhist priests known as *Vajrāchāryya,* few of the crowns seem to have survived. Of these, the present example is not only the best preserved, but unquestionably the finest. The four figures on the sides represent the four Tathāgatas, the fifth being symbolized by the thunderbolt (*vajra*) at the summit.

This sumptuously beautiful crown is an outstanding example of Nepali metalwork, in terms of both its bold design and its delicate execution. Not only is it a technical *tour de force,* but aesthetically it is a work of scintillating brilliance.

52. RESTORATION OF SVAYAMBHŪNĀTHA

Dated 1565
Opaque watercolor on cotton; H. 40½ in., W. 33½ *in.*
Lent anonymously

This remarkable painting shows the restoration of the stupa of Svayambhūnātha, which is one of the most prominent landmarks in the Kathmandu Valley. The restoration was undertaken during the lifetimes of the powerful noble Purandarasiṁha and his two brothers. While the focal point of the composition is the actual restoration of the stupa, carried out with an accompaniment of appropriate ceremonies and musical performances, the painting, in fact, provides us with a summary topographical chart of the entire valley, including the principal religious establishments.

Apart from its obvious historical significance, the painting is a striking visual statement, revealing both the artist's imaginative powers and his ability to organize what must have been a challenging composition. Obviously, design was of paramount importance, and it is remarkable how coherent and satisfying the composition is, despite the repetition of stereotyped motifs—architectural, figurative, and natural. With complete disregard for laws of perspective or gravity, the artist has succeeded brilliantly in combining these diverse shapes and forms in an exciting pictorial composition.

53. A STUPA

Eighteenth century
Gilt copper repoussé; H. 23¾ *in.,* W. 10 *in.*
Lent by the Asian Art Museum of San Francisco;
The Avery Brundage Collection

This stupa is a miniature version of the countless stupas, made of brick or stone, that can be seen in monasteries and courtyards in all the principal towns of the Kathmandu Valley. Four guardian figures appear on the rather tall base. The enshrined figures on the hemispherical dome are four of the Five Tathāgatas. The fifth Tathāgata, Vairochana, is said to reside within the womb of the stupa. Very likely, the eyes represented on each side of the square base of the spire are those of Vairochana and symbolize his omniscience. The spire consists of thirteen rings, which are symbolic of the thirteen stages of attaining Buddhahood.

Published: P. Pal, "The Aiḍuka of *Vishnudharmottarapurāṇa* and Certain Aspects of Stūpa Symbolism," *Journal of the Indian Society of Oriental Art,* n.s. vol. IV, no. 1 (1971–72), pl. IX.

Brahmanical Art

54. *Śiva-liṅga; ninth century*
Gilt copper; H. 3 *in.,* W. 3 *in. (right)*

55. *Śiva-liṅga; dated* 1046
Bronze; H. 5 *in. (below)*

56. *A Śaiva Manuscript Cover; twelfth century*
Opaque watercolor on wood; H. 1¾ *in.,* L. 22½ *in. (opposite)*

57. *Śiva as the Supreme Teacher (Dakshiṇāmurti); ca.* 1450
Opaque watercolor on cotton; H. 32⅝ *in.,*
W. 27¼ *in. (opposite)*

58. *Śiva as the Supreme Beggar (Bhikshāṭanamūrti); sixteenth century*
Copper with traces of gilt; H. 9¼ *in. (above)*

61. *Ardhanārīśvara; tenth century*
Copper inlaid with semiprecious stones; H. 33 *in. (right)*

59. *Umā-Maheśvara; fourteenth century*
Gilt copper inlaid with semiprecious stones; H. *6¼ in. (below)*

60. *Vīṇādhara Śiva with Pārvatī; seventeenth century*
Gilt copper; H. *5 in. (opposite)*

62. *Śaiva Scroll; ca.* 1600
Opaque watercolor on cotton; H. 14½ *in.*, W. 72 *in.*

63. *Vaṭuka Bhairava; tenth century*
Gilt bronze; H. 10¼ *in.*

64. *Cemetery with a Bhairava Shrine; fourteenth century or earlier*
Copper alloy; H. 3½ *in.,* W. 5¼ *in.*

65. *Bhairava and Śakti; dated 1784*
Gilt bronze with paint; H. *15¾ in. (opposite)*

66. *Bhairava; eighteenth century*
Gilt copper repoussé; H. *16½ in. (above)*

67. *Head of Bhairava; eighteenth century*
Gilt bronze with semiprecious stones and paint;
H. 30 *in.*, W. 36 *in. (opposite)*

68. *Śrīkaṇṭha Kāmakalā; eighteenth century*
Gilt bronze; H. 12 *in. (detail at right)*

69. *A Goddess; ninth century*
Gilt copper; H. 12 *in. (below)*

70. *Vārāhī; thirteenth–fourteenth century*
Gilt copper; H. 8½ *in. (opposite)*

71. *The Goddess Guhyakālī; fifteenth century*
Gilt copper; H. 14 *in. (below)*

72. *The Goddess Guhyakālī; seventeenth century*
Opaque watercolor on cotton; H. 64 *in.*, W. 51 *in. (opposite)*

73. *Durgā Killing Mahishāsura; sixteenth century*
Gilt bronze inlaid with semiprecious stones; H. 11½ *in.,* W. 13 *in. (above)*

74. *Folio from a Devīmāhātmya; eighteenth century*
Opaque watercolor on paper; H. 4⅝ *in.,* W. 8⅛ *in. (opposite, below)*

75. *Dancing Pārvatī; seventeenth century*
Gilt bronze; H. 12¼ *in. (opposite, above)*

76. *Sarasvatī; ca.* 1500
Gilt copper; H. 8¼ *in.,* W. 5½ *in. (opposite)*

77. *Sarasvatī (or Brahmāṇī); sixteenth century*
Gilt copper; H. 7 *in.,* W. 5½ *in. (above right)*

78. *Vishṇu; tenth century*
Gilt bronze; H. 8½ *in.,* W. 5 *in. (below left)*

79. *Vishṇu Riding on Garuḍa; dated* 1004
Gilt copper repoussé; H. 17 *in.,* W. 11 *in. (below right)*

80. *Vishṇu Mandala, by Tejarāma; dated* 1420
Opaque watercolor on cloth; H. 29¼ *in.,* W. 24¼ *in. (left)*

81. *Vishṇu Mandala; dated* 1681
Opaque watercolor on cotton; H. 65$\frac{5}{16}$ *in.,* W. 50⅝ *in. (below, detail opposite)*

82. *Jalaśayana Vishṇu; seventeenth century*
Gilt bronze; L. 7¼ *in. (below left)*

83. *Vaishṇava Mandala; eighteenth century*
Gilt copper and precious stones; D. 35 *in. (opposite)*

84. *Krishṇa Fluting; fifteenth century*
Bronze; H. 7⅛ *in. (below right)*

a.

b.

85 a., b. *Two Folios from the Bhāgavata Purāṇa; eighteenth century*
Opaque watercolor on paper; H. 15 *in.,* W. 22 *in. each (opposite, detail below)*

86. *Garuḍa; fifteenth century*
Gilt bronze inlaid with semiprecious stones; H. *7 in. (above)*

87. *Indra; twelfth century*
Gilt copper inlaid with semiprecious stones; H. *10 in. (opposite)*

88. *Dancing Kumāra; fifteenth–sixteenth century*
Gilt copper; H. *6¼ in. (right)*

89. *Dancing Kumāra; seventeenth century. Gilt copper;* H. 6½ *in.*

90. *Dancing Gaṇeśa; seventeenth century. Gilt copper;* H. 6¼ *in.*

91. *Dancing Figure; fourteenth–fifteenth century*
Copper alloy; H. 3¾ *in. (left)*

92. *A Serpent-king (Nāgarāja); ca.* 1500
Gilt bronze inlaid with semiprecious stones; H. 14 *in. (opposite)*

93. *Opium Pipe; sixteenth century or earlier*
Bronze with green patina; L. 8 *in. (below)*

a. (exterior)

b. (exterior)

94 a., b. *Pair of Manuscript Covers; seventeenth century. Opaque watercolor and gold on wood;* H. 4½ *in.*, W. 10 *in.*

a. (interior)

b. (interior)

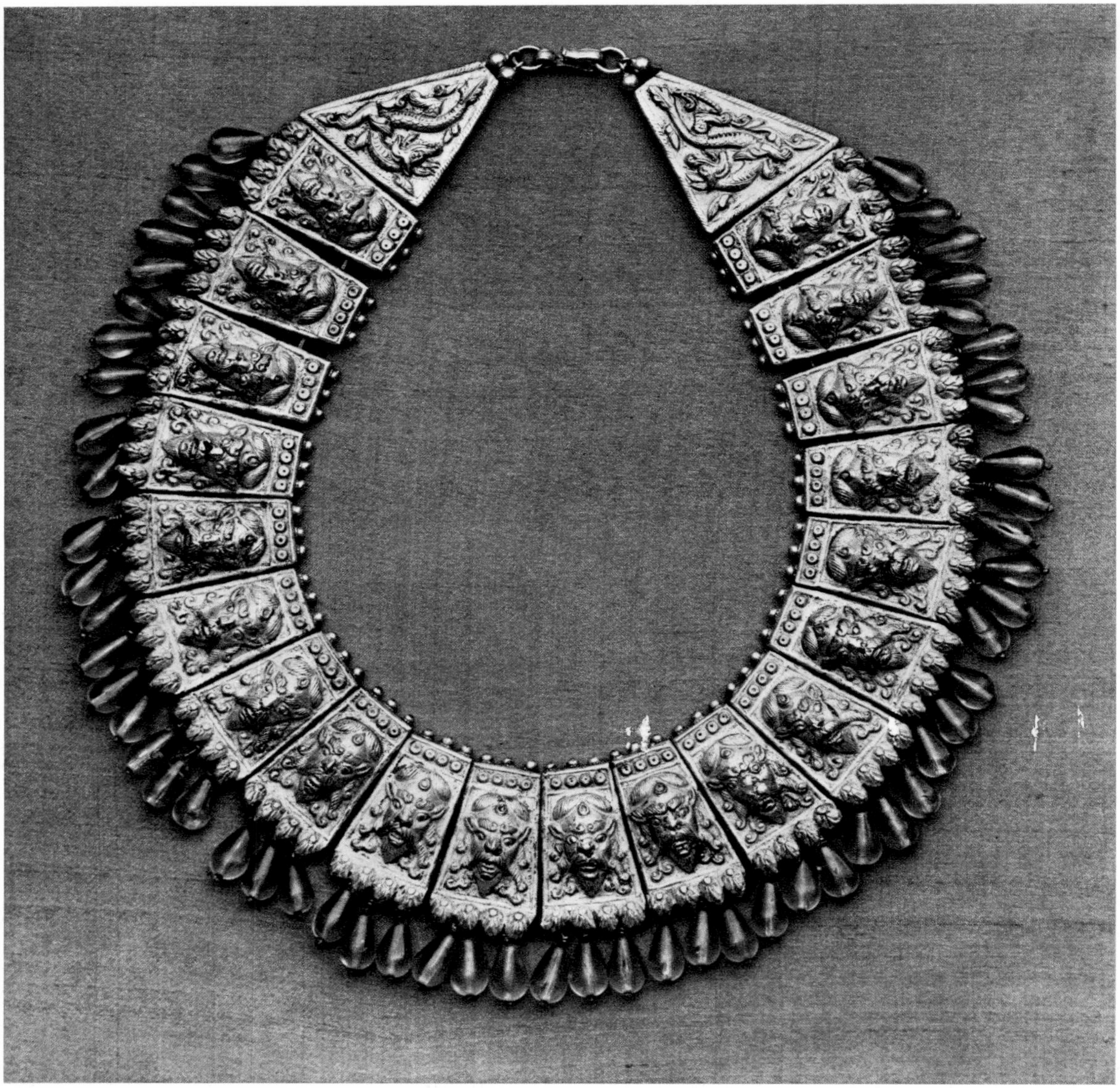

95. *Necklace; eighteenth century*
Gilt copper with glass pendants; D. 8¾ *in. (above)*

96. *Lamp with Devotees; dated* 1821
Brass; H. 8⅞ *in. (opposite)*

54. ŚIVA-LIṄGA

Ninth century
Gilt copper; H. 3 *in.,* W. 3 *in.*
Lent by Doris Wiener

A *liṅga* or *liṅgam* is the phallic emblem of Śiva and is used to represent him more often than any other symbol. This particular example probably served as an encasement for a stone linga. Such lingas, where the heads and hands of four figures are modeled in high relief on the four cardinal sides, are known as *chaturmukha* ("four-faced") *liṅga*. The faces symbolize four of the five fundamental aspects of Śiva, which are equated with the five elements. Thus, Sadyojāta symbolizes the earth, Vāmadeva water, Aghora light, and Tatpurusha air. The fifth aspect, Iśāṇa (also known as Sadāśiva), is represented by the aniconic dome of the linga and equated with the sky. One of the faces, that of Aghora, represents the angry aspect of the deity. The hands of each figure hold a rosary and a water pot.

Despite the diminutive size of the heads, it is remarkable how sensitively the features are delineated. The physiognomy is strongly reminiscent of faces seen on Śiva-liṅgas of the Gupta period, therefore an early date is being suggested for this bronze. It is certainly earlier than the Eilenberg Śiva-liṅga (No. 55), which was consecrated in the year 1046 A.D.

Published: P. Pal, "Three Dated Nepali Bronzes and Their Stylistic Significance," *Archives of Asian Art*, vol. XXV (1971–72), p. 63, fig. 11; Pal, *The Arts of Nepal*, vol. I, fig. 123.

55. ŚIVA-LIṄGA

Dated 1046
Bronze; H. 5 *in.*
Lent by Dr. Samuel Eilenberg

Unlike the previous example (No. 54), this linga is placed within a container for liquid, or *jalahāri*. The original purpose of the spouted container was to drain off the liquids that were poured over the linga as part of a ritual bath. Later, however, due to the strong emergence of the Śakti cult, the container came to be regarded as the *yonī*, the female sex symbol. This linga, which rises from a lotus, has also been provided with four faces. It may be pointed out, however, that none of the faces emphasizes Śiva's angry aspect.

Because of a dedicatory inscription, indicating that it was consecrated in the year 1046 when King Bhāskaradera was on the throne, the bronze is of considerable significance for the history of Nepali art.

Published: Pal, "Three Dated Nepali Bronzes . . . ," p. 62, figs. 7–10; Pal, *The Arts of Nepal*, vol. I, fig. 32.

56. A ŚAIVA MANUSCRIPT COVER

Twelfth century
Opaque watercolor on wood; H. 1¾ *in.,* L. 22½ *in.*
Lent by Mr. and Mrs. John Gilmore Ford

This cover probably once belonged to a Śaiva text such as the *Śivadharma Purāṇa*. In the center a *mukhaliṅga*, symbolizing Śiva (see Nos. 54, 55), is being worshipped by Brahmā and Vishṇu. Both these gods are accompanied by their wives. The eight remaining figures represent the eight Dikpālas, or guardians of the cardinal and intermediate directions. All the figures sit in a relaxed manner and are treated naturalistically. Although the style is essentially linear, the artist has skillfully conveyed a sense of volume. A comparison with the contemporary *Pañcharakshā* manuscript covers (No. 44) in the Binney Collection will at once make it apparent that Buddhist and Brahmanical manuscript illuminations are fundamentally similar.

Published: Pal, *Indo-Asian Art*, fig. 62.

57. ŚIVA AS THE SUPREME TEACHER *(Dakshiṇāmurti)*

Ca. 1450
Opaque watercolor on cotton; H. 32⅝ *in.,* W. 27¼ *in.*
Lent by Mr. and Mrs. John Gilmore Ford

Here Śiva appears as a pale yellow figure with a beard and matted hair, seated in the center of the painting in the yogic posture called *utkuṭikāsana*, with a piece of cloth known as a *yogapaṭṭa* tied around his legs. Since the god is represented as a teacher of yoga, his right hands display the gesture of exposition and the rosary, while the left hands hold the trident and the waterpot. He is surrounded by seventeen other yogis; each with two arms and each displaying different emblems or gestures. Other Brahmanical deities, the eight guardians, and the twelve signs of the zodiac complete the pantheon.

According to the inscription just above the bottom register, the painting was consecrated on the occasion of the performance of *Agastyavrata*, a Śaiva rite honoring the ancient sage Agastya. The fact that there is a waterpot immediately below the central figure probably indicates that the sage Agastya (who is said to have emerged from a pot) is identified here with Śiva himself.

Unfortunately the date as well as the reigning king's name have been removed. Stylistically, however, this painting is closely related to the 1420 Vishṇu mandala (No. 80). As in the Vasudhārā painting (No. 43), a rich and brilliant red predominates. The caves within which the yogis sit are imaginatively constructed with geometric rocks of green, yellow, and blue which sparkle like gems. Along with the delicate, lacy floral design of the arch, the colorful rocks enliven the composition and imbue the painting with dreamlike buoyancy.

Published: Pal, *Indo-Asian Art*, p. 47, fig. 63.

58. ŚIVA AS THE SUPREME BEGGAR *(Bhikshāṭanamūrti)*
Sixteenth century
Copper with traces of gilt; H. 9¼ *in.*
Lent by Mr. and Mrs. Jack Zimmerman

The story is told in the ancient Indian texts that once when Brahmā refused to admit Śiva's supremacy, Śiva cut off one of Brahmā's five heads in anger. Because it was a cardinal sin to destroy a brahmin, Śiva was cursed to roam around the universe as a beggar, carrying the skull from the severed head of Brahmā. This type of image, which symbolizes the incident, shows Śiva as a naked beggar.

Although the Bhikshāṭana images of Śiva are far more prevalent in South India than in the north, the appearance of this iconic form in Nepali art may be attributed to the growing influence of Śaiva brahmins in Nepal after the fourteenth century. In the usual South Indian representations, the face is that of a benign god. Here, however, the visage is forbidding and resembles that of a Bhairava (see Nos. 65, 66). Even more unusual is the hieratic posture of the figure, which creates a particularly imposing effect because of the curious disposition of the two upper arms. The body is that of a naked youth—a suitable form for the divine beggar who charmed the wives of the sages as he went begging from door to door.

59. UMĀ-MAHEŚVARA
Fourteenth century
Gilt copper inlaid with semiprecious stones; H. 6¼ *in.*
Lent by the Pan-Asian Collection

Of all the Śaiva themes represented in Nepali sculpture, the one known as Umā-Maheśvara is by far the most popular. In such icons Śiva (Maheśvara) and his consort, Pārvatī (Umā), are usually portrayed seated beside each other in a relaxed, affectionate posture, as in this example. With his upper hands, Śiva holds the rosary and the trident; the lower right hand displays the gesture of exposition, and the remaining left hand caresses Umā's breast. Umā leans gracefully against Śiva and holds a lotus with her left hand. Rather curious is the disposition of Umā's lion under Śiva's right foot.

Except for Śiva's additional arms, the delineation is essentially human. Śiva and Pārvatī have remained the divine exemplars of human love, and the Nepali artists have particularly emphasized this intimate relationship between the two, not only by compositional means, but also by imbuing the figures with soft sensuousness and languorous grace.

60. VĪṆĀDHARA ŚIVA WITH PĀRVATĪ
Seventeenth century
Gilt copper; H. 5 *in.*
Lent by Mr. and Mrs. Eric D. Morse

It is evident that this image reflects further iconographic elaborations of the Umā-Maheśvara theme (No. 59). Śiva is here given eighteen arms and, significantly, his principal hands are engaged in playing a lute, or *vīṇā*. Hence in this form he is known as Vīṇādhara Śiva. It may be pointed out that Śiva is regarded as the original teacher (*ādiguru*) of both music and dance.

The additional arms are disposed in such a manner that the outline of the bronze makes almost a complete circle. This enhances the circular flow of movement and compensates for the somewhat hieratic rigidity of the figures, especially that of Pārvatī. The bronze is attached to a piece of wood from the building that it once graced.

61. ARDHANĀRĪŚVARA
Tenth century
Copper inlaid with semiprecious stones; H. 33 *in.*
Lent by the Los Angeles County Museum of Art;
The Nasli and Alice Heeramaneck Collection

When Śiva and Pārvatī are portrayed androgynously, as in this figure, the form is known as *ardhanārīśvara*. Usually the left half of the figure represents the female, Pārvatī, and the right half the male, Śiva. Such androgynous forms were conceived by the theologians to emphasize the bisexuality, and therefore the nonduality, of the supreme being. The two halves are clearly distinguished, not only by anatomical differences, but also by their garments and ornaments. One of the right hands is broken and the other holds a trident upside down. The upper left hand probably held a mirror, a symbol of feminine vanity; the lower left hand holds a pot.

In terms of the modeling and slim proportions, the bronze is comparable to the Maitreya in the Pan-Asian Collection (No. 14) and to the near-contemporary Tārā (No. 37). The Ardhanārīśvara is marked by the same svelte elegance and classic simplicity as the others. Especially appealing is the gentle and tranquil expression of the face, which enhances the spiritual quality of the image.

Published: *The Arts of India and Nepal; Heeramaneck Collection*, p. 83; Pal, *The Arts of Nepal*, vol. I, fig. 150.

62. ŚAIVA SCROLL
Ca. 1600
Opaque watercolor on cotton; H. 14½ *in.*, W. 72 *in.*
Lent by Mr. Stephen T. Eckerd

This scroll illustrates a Śaiva myth associated with a *vrata*, or religious rite. The story unfolds from left to right, in two registers, and as is typical of Nepali scroll paintings, the incidents are portrayed in separate compositional segments. At the beginning (upper left), we see Śiva and Pārvatī playing a game of dice; next follow several scenes in which a man named Vaḍava is attacked in the ocean by sea monsters. Then the appearances of such gods as Indra, Kumāra, Kubera, and dancing Gaṇeśa are shown in several compartments. Finally, Vaḍava engages in performing the rite, the auspicious god Vināyaka (Gaṇeśa) appears before him, and Vaḍava is redeemed.

Several other scroll and manuscript paintings executed in this rather flamboyant style are known. There seems reason to believe that the style, whose distinctive manner reflects the individuality of a particular artist and his school, was developed sometime in the second half of the sixteenth century and was localized in the town of Bhaktapur. The style is substantially different from the earlier narrative painting tradition (see No. 43), or from those of other contemporary works.

63. VAṬUKA BHAIRAVA

Tenth century
Gilt bronze; H. 10¼ *in.*
Lent by Doris Wiener

Bhairava is the common appellation for Śiva's angry or ferocious form, the form he assumes in order to destroy evil. The word *vaṭuka* further qualifies the figure as a dwarf. This is not only a rare representation of Vaṭuka Bhairava, but may be the earliest known. His squat, rotund body is covered with unusually active snakes and he wears an elephant's hide as a mantle. His anger is expressed both by his glaring eyes and by the gesture of admonition he makes with one of his left hands. The emblems in his other hands are a skull-cup, a battle-axe, and an elephant goad. The artist's sense of baroque exuberance is revealed in the treatment of the garments, the snakes, and the elephant hide, and also in the peculiar manner of delineating the two weapons in the upper hands. The hair is elegantly arranged and the head, with its snake crown, is haloed by a nimbus of flames that is typical of the period.

Published: Pal, *The Arts of Nepal*, vol. I, fig. 151.

64. CEMETERY WITH A BHAIRAVA SHRINE

Fourteenth century or earlier
Copper alloy; H. 3½ *in.*, W. 5¼ *in.*
Lent by the Pan-Asian Collection

A bronze of unusual interest, this piece shows a Bhairava shrine in a cremation ground. In the foreground we see a body being cremated, and immediately behind that is a barking dog that obviously occupies the place of eminence. The dog is the mount of Bhairava and is often substituted for the god himself. He is flanked by two of the scavenging birds which usually inhabit such cremation grounds. That the dog is intended to be enshrined is evident from the four posts surrounding him, which must have supported a roof. On one side of the originally covered area is a snake and on the other is a stunted tree.

The shrine is surrounded by five figures, a linga, and a stupa. The figures, crowned and ornamented, are seated in yogic postures. The one at the front left corner has four heads, but the others are all normal human representations. Each holds a weapon with his left hand and raises his right hand to his mouth in a gesture implying silence (*maunavrata*). The multiple heads of the one figure clearly indicate that they are all to be regarded as divine rather than human beings. They probably represent the five forms of Śiva that are equated with the five elements (*pañchabhūta*). Finally, the inclusion of both the stupa and the linga indicates that the shrine is venerated by Buddhists as well as Śaivas.

65. BHAIRAVA AND ŚAKTI

Dated 1784
Gilt bronze with paint; H. 15¾ *in.*
Lent by the Los Angeles County Museum of Art;
gift of The Ahmanson Foundation

This remarkable bronze portrays Śiva as Bhairava, accompanied by his Śakti, Pārvatī. Striking a militant posture, he bestrides two crawling human beings as sixteen of his eighteen arms brandish a variety of weapons in a convincing demonstration of his physical powers. His awesomeness is further emphasized by the angry miens of his five heads, his skull garlands and tiaras, and his beloved snakes. Rather curiously, a sixth head appears on the lotus base—a feature not encountered in any other such icon. In contrast with the large, ferocious image of Śiva, his Śakti seems particularly small and dainty, as she stands in a dancing posture on her mount, the lion.

Cast in several pieces and fitted together with great skill, the bronze is an extraordinary example of both the technical dexterity and the visual imagination of the Newari artists. The repeated application of vermillion, much of which still adheres to the surface, not only gives the gilding an attractive texture, but also enhances the mystical appeal of the figure for the devotee.

66. BHAIRAVA

Eighteenth century
Gilt copper repoussé; H. 16½ *in.*
Lent anonymously

The striding god has four heads and three pairs of arms. His rotund belly is given added emphasis by the serpent that serves as a sacred cord. In addition to his conventional ornaments, he sports a bone apron and an animal skin which is meant to be that of a tiger, but looks more like that of a bear. Except for the lotus, the noose, and the bell, the emblems in his hands are not clearly recognizable. The other three objects, however, are certainly weapons. Rather unusual is the inclusion of the lotus, which is not a common attribute of Bhairava.

A cursory comparison will make it apparent that this representation is substantially different from the Los Angeles Bhairava (No. 65), in terms of both style and iconography. Despite his more violent gestures and posture, this Bhairava image is not particularly forbidding. Instead, the portrayal is characterized by a sense of whimsy that is especially evident in the delineation of the curious animal skin.

67. HEAD OF BHAIRAVA
Eighteenth century
Gilt bronze with semiprecious stones and paint; H. 30 *in.*, W. 36 *in.*
Lent by Mr. and Mrs. Jack Zimmerman

This large and impressive head of Bhairava probably adorned an entrance to a shrine. Such heads are often referred to, without any foundation, as masks, and are a familiar feature of Nepali religious architecture. However, they are more commonly made of wood. A curious application of a similar head may be seen in the bronze image of Bhairava and Śakti (No. 65). In terms of stylized grandeur and love of whimsy, such sculptures are comparable to the equally imaginative, though more theatrical, demon heads of Cambodia and Java.

68. ŚRĪKAṆṬHA KĀMAKALĀ
Eighteenth century
Gilt bronze; H. 12 *in.*
Lent by Mr. and Mrs. Jack Zimmerman

A rare tantric manifestation of Śiva known as Śrīkaṇṭha, or "the one with the beautiful throat," is the subject of this complex bronze. Both the god and his partner are shown dancing and they are also engaged in copulation, hence this type of image is described in iconographic texts as *kāmakalā*. Both deities are provided with multiple heads and arms, and below their feet are two figures who support the lotuses on which the divine feet are placed. On the next tier a bull and a lion flank a corpse. Lower still is a row of five figures symbolizing the five basic elements that constitute the phenomenal world.

What is remarkable about such works is not only how they reflect the bizarre imagination of tantric theologians, but also how adroitly the artist has translated such concepts into pleasing aesthetic forms. While we admire the artist's sense of balance and design, we are also struck by the technical dexterity required to cast this unusually intricate bronze.

69. A GODDESS
Ninth century
Gilt copper; H. 12 *in.*
Lent by the Pan-Asian Collection

Isolated as she is, the exact identification of this figure remains unclear. From her posture, however, it can be determined that she once sat beside a male companion. Very likely her companion was Śiva and hence she can be tentatively identified as Pārvatī, or Umā (compare No. 59). Whatever her identification, she remains one of the most exciting realizations of the female form in Nepali sculpture. Although her form is idealized, it is at the same time imbued with delightfully natural rhythm and sensuous grace. She is both relaxed and provocative, and her physical abundance is informed with majestic elegance. The turn of the head and the expression on her face, displaying just a touch of conceit, add to the strongly human qualities of the sculpture. It is as if the sculptor had used a beautiful, proud queen as his model.

70. VĀRĀHĪ
Thirteenth–fourteenth century
Gilt copper; H. 8½ *in.*
Lent by Mr. and Mrs. Eric D. Morse

With her boar's head and rather rotund form, Vārāhī, who is regarded as one of the Mother goddesses, is obviously the female counterpart of the Boar incarnation (Varāha-avatāra) of Vishṇu. Seated gracefully, she displays a noose, a fish, a skull-cup, and the gesture of exposition. Her generous form has been modeled with sensual elegance and the beautiful locks of hair that cascade down over her shoulders are especially noteworthy. The goddess is still attached to a piece of wood from the original temple where she was once housed. Although the building was apparently destroyed in 1934, in an earthquake, the image not only survived, but is remarkably well-preserved.

71. THE GODDESS GUHYAKĀLĪ
Fifteenth century
Gilt copper; H. 14 *in.*
Lent by James D. Thornton

The goddess Kālī is especially venerated in Nepal and one of her most interesting forms is that known as Guhyakālī, which literally means "secret or hidden Kālī." The consort, or Śakti, of Paśupatinātha, a manifestation of Śiva and the national god of the country, Guhyakālī, is generally represented in an aniconic form. Her iconic representations are extremely rare, which makes the two examples included in this exhibition (see also No. 72) especially interesting.

The composition sets forth Guhyakālī's complex iconography in an admirable fashion. Despite her multiple, grotesque heads, her multiple limbs, and the forbidding bone apron, the goddess remains a desirable woman. Indeed, in contrast to the awesome animal heads, her human head displays a serene mien. The Nepali artists were especially adept at combining the grotesque and the beautiful into visually exciting compositions such as this. The dog, it may be noted, is the animal associated with Śiva in his Bhairava manifestation.

72. THE GODDESS GUHYAKĀLĪ

Seventeenth century
Opaque watercolor on cotton; H. 64 *in.*, W. 51 *in.*
Lent by Mr. and Mrs. Jack Zimmerman

In this exceptionally large painting, the iconography of the goddess Guhyakālī (No. 71) is even more complex. She is portrayed with a thousand arms and four legs, dancing ecstatically against a sea of orange and red flames. The additional arms radiate from the body in a symmetrical fashion to form an aureole; the many heads are beautifully arranged in a pyramid. Provided with two dogs as her mounts, the goddess also tramples upon several deities. Other Śaiva deities are portrayed elsewhere in the painting and in two tiers along the pedestal. On either side of the goddess, the eight cemeteries are delineated against the alternating blue and green ground.

73. DURGĀ KILLING MAHISHĀSURA

Sixteenth century
Gilt bronze inlaid with semiprecious stones; H. 11½ *in.*, W. 13 *in.*
Lent by Dorothy and Ernst Payer

This elaborate bronze shows the Brahmanical goddess Durgā killing Mahishāsura, the buffalo demon, after he has changed his form numerous times in order to escape her wrath. Provided with eighteen arms, Durgā brandishes various weapons given to her by the gods, as she stands in a militant posture with her right foot on her lion and her left on the buffalo's back. The decapitated head of the buffalo lies between her feet, and the *asura* (demon) emerging from the animal's body is about to unsheath his sword. At each end of the pedestal, a companion of the *asura* kneels on a rock base, holding a sword and a mace.

So elaborate and complete a bronze representation of the theme is rare. Especially interesting are the addition of the two attendant *asuras* and the remarkably naturalistic delineation of the buffalo's head. Noteworthy also are the exquisitely rendered vegetal motifs along the front of the base. Despite such embellishments, however, the composition is characterized by clarity and simple elegance.

74. FOLIO FROM A DEVĪMĀHĀTMYA

Eighteenth century
Opaque watercolor on paper; H. 4⅝ *in.*, W. 8⅛ *in.*
Lent by Mr. Paul F. Walter

In a delightfully imaginative battle scene a stiff Durgā is engaged in combat with equally stiff and puppet-like *asuras* (demons). There is little difference in the facial expressions between the decapitated heads of the *asuras* and those still on their shoulders. Arms and legs float around freely and blood flows abundantly. Rather interesting is the abstract treatment of rocks and peaks in the foreground. The folio is from a manuscript of the *Devīmāhātmya*, a text that extols the story of the goddess's battle with the forces of evil.

75. DANCING PĀRVATĪ

Seventeenth century
Gilt bronze; H. 12¼ *in.*
Lent by the Asian Art Museum of San Francisco;
The Avery Brundage Collection

Although the complementary figure has been lost, this dancing female was once paired with a dancing Śiva and hence must depict his consort, Pārvatī. The third eye marked clearly on her forehead corroborates the identification. Images of Pārvatī dancing are extremely rare, which makes this figure especially interesting. Both in terms of ornaments and dress the goddess reflects the fashions prevalent in seventeenth-century Nepal. As a matter of fact, the sculpture could be regarded as an idealized study of a court dancer.

76. SARASVATĪ

Ca. 1500
Gilt copper; H. 8¼ *in.*, W. 5½ *in.*
Lent by the Museum of Fine Arts, Boston;
purchase, Marshall H. Gould Fund

The deity in this beautiful sculpture represents the Brahmanical goddess, Sarasvatī. In reference to her role as goddess of wisdom and music, her upper left hand holds a manuscript and the two principal hands once played the *vīṇā* (see No. 60). Her remaining right hand must have displayed a now missing rosary. Richly ornamented and crowned, the goddess sits gracefully on a lotus in the posture known as *lalitāsana*. Attractive as the goddess is, the exquisitely rendered floriate scroll that encloses the figure without engulfing it is even more engaging. The openwork of the curling rhizome as well as the space around the goddess's figure are effective in creating a pleasing visual contrast between solid masses and empty space.

Published: Pal, *The Arts of Nepal*, vol. I, fig. 240.

77. SARASVATĪ (OR BRAHMĀṆĪ)
Sixteenth century
Gilt copper; H. 7 *in.*, W. 5½ *in.*
Lent by the Pan-Asian Collection

In this bronze we see an unusual representation of a goddess seated on a lotus in the yogic posture called *utkuṭikāsana* (see No. 57), with a *yogapaṭṭa* tied around her knees. She is clad and ornamented in the usual manner, wearing a jewelled necklace that emphasizes her firm breasts. The goddess's right hand displays the gesture of munificence (*varadamudrā*) and her left hand supports a waterpot. Below her left knee is a charming representation of a goose, or *haṁsa*.

There are two possible identifications of the figure, since the goose is the mount of both Brahmāṇī and Sarasvatī. Both the waterpot and the yogic posture could also relate to either deity. In the author's opinion, however, this image represents Sarasvatī rather than Brahmāṇī.

78. VISHṆU
Tenth century
Gilt bronze; H. 8½ *in.*, W. 5 *in.*
Lent by Mrs. George H. Bunting

Framed by a richly embellished aureole, Vishṇu, the second god of the Brahmanical triad, stands in a hieratic posture on a rectangular base. The front of the base is decorated with a vegetable motif. Vishṇu's four arms carry the wheel, the mace, the conch, and a boss symbolizing the lotus. As befits a king, he is elaborately crowned and ornamented with jewels. The elegance of the figure is greatly enhanced by the exquisitely rendered aureole and nimbus. On the inner curve, the aureole is decorated with a meandering vine scroll; the outer curve is edged with the ubiquitous flame motif. The nimbus is ornamented with a combined pearl and flame motif.

79. VISHṆU RIDING ON GARUḌA
Dated 1004
Gilt copper repoussé; H. 17 *in.*, W. 11 *in.*
Lent by Mr. and Mrs. Jack Zimmerman

According to the inscription at the bottom, this repoussé plaque was used to enclose a stone image that must have had the same form. The plaque is of great art-historical significance, because it is dated. It also reveals how early the repoussé technique was known in Nepal.

Vishṇu sits astride his half-avian, half-human mount, the Garuḍa, whose arms are spread out along his outstretched wings, thereby emphasizing the fact that he is in flight. As they radiate behind Vishṇu, Garuḍa's tail-feathers, which are curiously like those of a peacock, serve as an elaborate aureole. Vishṇu is accompanied by two adoring females, who must represent his two wives, Śrī-Lakshmī and Bhū-devī.

Published: Pal, "Three Dated Nepali Bronzes . . . ," p. 58, figs. 1 and 2; Pal, *The Arts of Nepal*, vol. I, fig. 30.

80. VISHṆU MANDALA
By Tejarāma
Dated 1420
Opaque watercolor on cloth; H. 29¼ *in.*, W. 24¼ *in.*
Lent by the Los Angeles County Museum of Art;
The Nasli and Alice Heeramaneck Collection

Brahmanical mandalas are quite rare and this example is especially important because it is the earliest dated specimen known. At the center of the lotus is the figure of Vishṇu, seated on the intertwined coils of the serpent-king Ananta, whose seven heads form a parasol over the god. Vishṇu is flanked by his consort Lakshmī and his mount Garuḍa. It may be noted that the center of the mandala coincides with the middle of Vishṇu's chest. The lotus has twelve petals, each containing an image of Vishṇu in one of his twenty-four emanations, with the corresponding Śakti. Outside the lotus are eight guardians of the four cardinal and four intermediary directions. In addition, each gateway of the mandala is guarded by a pair of ferocious deities who may represent Bhairavas (Nos. 63–67). Above the mandala are several other important members of the Brahmanical pantheon; below are scenes of ceremonial rituals and portraits of members of the donor's family.

The pattern of lines on the portion of Vishṇu's chest where the white pigment has peeled off clearly demonstrates the underlying geometric structure of the mandala. Since the iconography and color schemes of such mandalas were precisely defined, the visual appeal of an individual painting often depends upon its execution. In this instance we can hardly fail to admire the sure draftsmanship of the artist as well as his sensitive use of the brush in creating the rich, pleasing tonality of colors.

Apart from its significance as a dated work of art, this is one of the very few examples where the artist's name is included in the inscription. We are told that a certain Tejarāma was not only the donor of this painting, but was also responsible for executing it.

Published: *The Arts of India and Nepal: Heeramaneck Collection*, fig. 125.

81. VISHṆU MANDALA

Dated 1681
Opaque watercolor on cotton; H. 65⁹⁄₁₆ *in.*, W. 50⅝ *in.*
Lent by the Los Angeles County Museum of Art;
Acquisition Fund Purchase

Although substantially different from the preceding example, this painting may be regarded as a mandala. Here, the iconography is obviously far more complex and the mandala contains many more divinities. Of particular interest are the representations of the ten avatars of Vishṇu along the top, the twelve signs of the zodiac in the two vertical rows immediately flanking the central shrine, and the twenty-eight stars, or *nakshatras*, along the outer rows and along the tier just below the inscription.

This painting was dedicated on the occasion of the performance of *Avantavrata*, a Vaishṇava rite, during the reign of King Jitāmitramalla of Bhaktapur. The King, preceded by trumpeters, is portrayed in the lowermost register and is distinguished by the polycephalous serpent canopy behind him.

It would be impossible here to discuss the many interesting features, both iconographic and stylistic, offered by this painting. It is worth noting, however, that although the painting reveals a rich palette, the colors themselves are not as intense and sensuous as in the fifteenth-century work (No. 80). Of special interest is the intrusion of Mughal-Rajput elements evident in the delineation of the princely costumes and the winged angels.

82. JALAŚAYANA VISHṆU

Seventeenth century
Gilt bronze; L. 7¼ *in.*
Lent by the Pan-Asian Collection

The icon portraying Vishṇu sleeping on a bed of serpents in the cosmic ocean is known as Jalaśayana Vishṇu. In Nepal the cult of Jalaśayana Vishṇu is especially popular and there are several monumental examples. The most famous is the shrine of Buḍhānīlkanṭh, which was established in 642 A.D. and still continues to draw millions of worshippers each year. To the author's knowledge, this is the only bronze example of Jalaśayana Vishṇu from either Nepal or India that has come to light. The bronze is therefore of considerable iconographic significance. Furthermore, the braiding of the coil of the multi-hooded *nāga* appears to be uniquely Nepali.

83. VAISHṆAVA MANDALA

Eighteenth century
Gilt copper and precious stones; D. 35 *in.*
Lent by The Newark Museum;
Sophronia Anderson Bequest Fund

The Newari craftsmen have been renowned for decorative work combining the techniques of filigree, repoussé, and inlay. Few examples, however, are as sumptuous as this mandala. Not only is the workmanship of extraordinary precision, but the total visual effect is breathtakingly lavish. Hundreds of stones including rubies, pearls, amethysts, tourmalines, turquoises, and coral decorate the intricate design. The deities have been carved of transparent quartz, colored on the underside.

In the center of the mandala, Vishṇu and Lakshmī stand like two lovers. Vishṇu's blue complexion as well as his stance clearly indicate his identification with Krishṇa (see No. 84). Ten other figures, all blue, surround the divine couple, and the number coincides with the traditional number of Vishṇu's incarnations. Flying celestial beings flank the four gateways; the eight figures in the circular border represent the eight guardians.

Published: E. Olson, *Catalogue of the Tibetan Collection and Other Lamaist Material in the Newark Museum*, vol. III (Newark, 1971), frontispiece and p. 24.

84. KRISHṆA FLUTING

Fifteenth century
Bronze; H. 7⅛ *in.*
Lent by Mr. and Mrs. John Gilmore Ford

This bronze represents the cowherd-god Krishṇa in a classic pose that is as familiar as that of a dancing Śiva of India's Chola period. The crossed legs and the tilt of the head enhance the graceful posture. The two hands once held a flute which Krishṇa played in the pasturelands of Brindaban to charm the cowgirls. Especially noteworthy are the large, staring eyes and the absence of any ornamentation. Very likely the image, intended for a domestic altar, would have been clothed and adorned with suitable jewelry by its owner, as was the custom in Bengal. The bronze reveals strong influences of the better known and more numerous Bengali images of Krishṇa.

85. TWO FOLIOS FROM THE BHĀGAVATA PURĀṆA

Eighteenth century

Opaque watercolor on paper; H. 15 *in.,* W. 22 *in. each*

a) *Lent by Dr. Edwin Binney, 3rd*

b) *Lent by the Los Angeles County Museum of Art; gift of Michael J. Connell Foundation*

These folios are from a remarkable set of paintings illustrating sections of the Vaishṇava text, the *Bhāgavata Purāṇa.* Not only are the paintings of unusually large dimensions, but they also reveal the very individual style of a particular artist. Most of the folios in the set are similar to the Binney example (a), where there is a strong emphasis upon architecture. Indeed, the artist's obsession with architecture gives these paintings their distinctive character. In addition to juxtaposing many different forms of structures, he provides us with several views of palaces and buildings within a single visual field.

More unconventional is the Los Angeles folio (b). The scene depicts Krishṇa with his wife, descending from the sky and being welcomed by the lady of the house in the traditional manner. In keeping with the beliefs of the ancient cosmographers, the earth is drawn in the shape of a tortoise. Even more charming, however, is the actual landing of Krishṇa, riding his avian mount. Again the use of multiple perspective, and of a bird's-eye view of the entire scene, make the representation especially graphic.

86. GARUḌA

Fifteenth century

Gilt bronze inlaid with semiprecious stones; H. 7 *in.*

Lent by the Pan-Asian Collection

Vishṇu's mount, Garuḍa, began his career in Indian mythology as a sun-bird and an arch-enemy of the terrestrial serpents. He has remained a favorite subject among Indian sculptors and has been portrayed in an immense variety of forms, but his representations in Indonesia and Nepal are even more imaginative. For some reason, the Nepalis, who prefer to show him as a more anthropomorphic than avian figure, display a marked predilection for depicting him as a young boy.

In this delightfully decorative sculpture, not only does the creature strike an unusually dramatic posture, but there is also a quality of amusing fantasy. Although the body is that of a young boy, the chest is embellished with swirling forms that indicate thick tufts of hair. His face is a curious admixture of avian and demonic features, with a prominent beak and highly stylized eyebrows. Even more inventive are the vegetation-like forms of the wings and the feathers attached to the ankles.

Published: Pal, *The Arts of Nepal,* vol. I, fig. 107.

87. INDRA

Twelfth century

Gilt copper inlaid with semiprecious stones; H. 10 *in.*

Lent by Mr. and Mrs. John D. Rockefeller 3rd

The cult of Indra has remained more important in Nepal than in India, and a festival in his honor, when such images of the god are taken out of the temples and paraded in the streets, is still celebrated annually. It appears to be a non-sectarian festival enjoyed by both Hindus and Buddhists.

The principal identification mark of Indra is the third eye marked horizontally across his forehead, in contrast to the vertical third eye of Śiva. In both Hindu and Buddhist mythology, Indra is considered the king of the gods. Consequently, in Nepal he is always portrayed as a sumptuously adorned, regal figure, wearing a gem-encrusted crown of a distinctive shape. This figure is further distinguished by the posture in which he sits: one befitting an indulgent, relaxed, and graceful monarch. Indeed, few Nepali Indras convey a sense of majesty as well as does this image.

Published: S. E. Lee, *Asian Art, Part II: Selections from the Collection of Mr. and Mrs. John D. Rockefeller 3rd* (New York: Asia House Gallery, 1975), p. 20 and no. 7.

88. DANCING KUMĀRA

Fifteenth–sixteenth century

Gilt copper; H. 6¼ *in.*

Lent by The St. Louis Art Museum; purchase, W. K. Bixby Oriental Art Fund

Kumāra appears originally to have been a Yaksha, or tutelary spirit, of malevolent nature. Subsequently he was adopted into the Brahmanical pantheon as the son of Śiva and Pārvatī, and he has remained an endearing figure in Indian literature and mythology ever since. While in mythology he figures primarily as the general of the gods, in secular literature he is cast more as a mischievous child. It is this aspect of Kumāra's character that seems to have inspired some of the most charming representations of the god in Nepal, including this image of a plump, well-fed boy dancing merrily as his adoring peacock watches.

89. DANCING KUMĀRA

Seventeenth century

Gilt copper; H. 6½ *in.*

Lent by the Pan-Asian Collection

This dancing Kumāra figure is altogether different from the St. Louis image (No. 88). Here he is portrayed not as a boy, but as an awesome guardian figure with a round belly and bulging eyes. It is also unusual that he dances on the outspread wings of his peacock.

Obviously this bronze represents a tantric form of the god and hence he is given a third eye and four arms. Three of the hands carry a thunderbolt, a lance, and a waterpot, while the fourth displays the gesture of reassurance. Kumāra's head is set off by a flaming nimbus, and both he and his bird are beautifully framed by a larger aureole of flames.

90. DANCING GAṆEŚA

Seventeenth century
Gilt copper; H. 6¼ *in.*
Lent by the Pan-Asian Collection

Companion piece to the dancing Kumāra (No. 89), is this image of Gaṇeśa, the symbol of auspiciousness and another son of Śiva and Pārvatī. Gaṇeśa, too, dances on a mount, but it is his mother's lion rather than his usual mount, a mouse. That this image is tantric in nature is indicated by the multiple heads and arms, which are pleasingly arranged. Despite additional limbs and his own bulk, the movement of Gaṇeśa's dance, like that of his brother, Kumāra, is expressed with grace and buoyancy. Equally charming is the whimsical delineation of the lion with its upturned tail and humorous face.

91. DANCING FIGURE

Fourteenth–fifteenth century
Copper alloy; H. 3¾ *in.*
Lent by Mr. and Mrs. Jack Zimmerman

Since this bronze obviously has been detached from a larger group, its original context is not clear. It probably represents an attendant celestial being. The figure's altogether human expression and dancing posture convey a sense of joyous ecstasy. Despite the diminutive scale, it remains one of the liveliest Nepali bronzes in this assemblage.

92. A SERPENT-KING (NĀGARĀJA)

Ca. 1500
Gilt bronze inlaid with semiprecious stones; H. 14 *in.*
Lent by Mr. and Mrs. John Gilmore Ford

That the figure represents a serpent-king (Nāgarāja) is evident from the polycephalous hood emerging from his head. His regal character is also emphasized by the abundance of ornaments that adorn his body. From his attitude it is apparent that he is engaged in adoring a deity and he may well have been attached to the pedestal of a Buddha image. Whatever the original function of the image, from a purely aesthetic viewpoint this is one of the finest portrayals of a Nāgarāja that has come to light in Nepal. Dynamic in its expression of physical energy, it is also an inspired statement of rapturous ecstasy.

Published: Pal, *Indo-Asian Art*, fig. 56; Pal, *The Arts of Nepal*, vol. I, fig. 254; Pal, "Bronzes of Nepal," fig. 10.

93. OPIUM PIPE

Sixteenth century or earlier
Bronze with green patina; L. 8 *in.*
Lent by Dr. Samuel Eilenberg

Judging by the size of the bowl, this pipe was probably used for smoking opium. It also seems clear that it was used for ritual purposes, because the bowl is conceived as a lotus with two divine heads rendered in high relief. The stem is embellished with two dragons whose form, essentially Chinese, must have entered the Nepali artist's repertoire by way of Tibet. This is the only example of such a metal pipe known to the author. The green patina, rarely seen on Nepali bronzes, would indicate that the piece was buried in the ground for some time.

94. PAIR OF MANUSCRIPT COVERS

Seventeenth century
Opaque watercolor and gold on wood; H. 4½ *in.*, W. 10 *in.*
Lent anonymously

Both of these manuscript covers are illustrated inside as well as outside in a particularly vivid and lively style. On the exterior of one cover is a representation of a dancing Gaṇeśa with his consort and on the other is depicted the goddess Sarasvatī, which clearly indicates that the covers must have belonged to a Brahmanical manuscript. On the reverse side of the Sarasvatī painting, however, we see a Buddhist priest greeting a pair of richly caparisoned elephants, while the illustration on the interior of the other cover shows a second priest expounding to an enthroned king. More significant, from a religious point of view, is the curious figure of a deity shown in a vignette between the king and the priest. The figure is unquestionably the red form of Lokeśvara, worshipped as Matsyendranātha in Nepal, but oddly enough, the three animals below him are the mounts of Śiva, Brahmā, and Vishṇu. Thus the representation reflects the syncretic spirit that characterizes the religious climate in Nepal.

Equally interesting, from an iconographic viewpoint, are the representations of Sarasvatī and Gaṇeśa. Sarasvatī is given both a *makara* (sea monster) and a goose as her mounts, and she plays the musical instrument, *vīṇā*. Gaṇeśa's portrayal is remarkably naturalistic and spirited. His Śaiva affiliation is emphasized not only by the crescent-moon on his crown, the snake ornaments, and the tiger skin, but also by the fact that his consort is given the lion as a mount, thereby clearly implying that she is a form of Durgā. To Gaṇeśa's right, Śiva is shown dancing on his bull; to his left, Bhairava dances on a man. Both are also playing upon drums to provide the rhythm for Gaṇeśa's performance.

95. NECKLACE

Eighteenth century
Gilt copper with glass pendants; D. 8¾ *in.*
Lent anonymously

The women of Nepal are especially fond of jewelry and the Newari craftsman delights in creating beautiful necklaces, bangles, and anklets for his patrons. Most of the ornaments are embellished with inlay and filigree in very much the same technique as was used in making the Vishṇu mandala (No. 83) and the shrine (No. 13). This handsome necklace is included in the exhibition as a superb example of repoussé work and because of its unusual design of identical heads portrayed in high relief on each of the oblong sections. The exact significance or origin of this motif is unknown. The presence of the third eye on the forehead seems to indicate that the head is that of Bhairava, but the shape of the head, the arrangement of the hair, and the inclusion of a goatee are unusual. The two dragons are motifs borrowed from Tibetan art.

96. LAMP WITH DEVOTEES

Dated 1821
Brass; H. 8⅞ *in.*
Lent by The Denver Art Museum; Guthrie-Goodwin Collection

Lamps, which play a vital role in the religious rituals of Nepal both in homes and in temples, have often inspired artists to be inventive, but have received little or no attention as artistic forms. Although these lamps are almost always adorned with an image of a deity, this unusual example includes a group of portraits. The male in the middle represents the deceased father of the donor; the two females are his mother and stepmother. It is evident, however, that the portraits are essentially idealized and probably did not bear any physical likeness to the persons they depict.

Published: Pal, *The Arts of Nepal*, vol. I, fig. 49.

97. FOLIO FROM A NĀYIKĀ SERIES

Ca. 1650
Opaque watercolor on paper; H. 7$\frac{1}{16}$ *in.,* W. 5⅝ *in.*
Lent by the Los Angeles County Museum of Art;
Acquisitions Fund Purchase *illus. p.* 19

Nāyaka-Nāyikā bheda (Differentiation of Heroes and Heroines) is a familiar theme in the Indian rhetorical and artistic traditions. The heroes and heroines are archetypal lovers and the poetry usually describes particular situations in love. That the tradition reached Nepal is evident from this set of paintings, which stylistically seem to derive from the Mewar school of Rajput painting, but at the same time clearly announce the unknown Nepali artist's flair for originality.

The heroine in this painting is referred to as *Svādhina-bhartrikā*, an epithet indicating that her lover or husband is completely under her control. The mood is one of conjugal harmony. The bold hero, while pretending to feed her a betel leaf (*pān*), attempts to touch her breast. The demure lady makes a halfhearted gesture to dissuade him.

Although this is ostensibly a secular work, the curious manner in which the entire scene has been placed upon a lotus base shows that the artist was more accustomed to executing religious paintings. In both Buddhist and Brahmanical works, the gods are frequently represented on lotuses (see Nos. 32, 48 and 80, for example). Furthermore, in the literature and the paintings of this period, the *nāyaka* usually was identified with the god Krishṇa and the *nāyikā* with his consort, Rādhā.

Published: P. Pal, "Eight Heroines from Nepal," *Los Angeles County Museum of Art Bulletin 1974*, vol. XX, no. 2, p. 60, fig. 8.

SELECTED BIBLIOGRAPHY

Ancient Nepal, Journal of the Department of Archaeology, Kathmandu, nos. 1–10 (1967–1970).

The Arts of India and Nepal: The Nasli and Alice Heeramaneck Collection, Boston, 1966.

Arts of Asia, IV, 5 (September–October 1974).

BARRETT, D. "The Buddhist Art of Tibet and Nepal," *Oriental Art*, n.s. III, 3 (Summer 1957), pp. 90–95.

BROWN, P. *Picturesque Nepal*. London, 1912.

GOETZ, H. "Arte del Nepal," *La Civilita dell Oriente*, IV, Rome, 1962.

———. *Studies in the History and Art of Kashmir and the Indian Himalayas*. Wiesbaden, 1969.

LIU, I-SE (ed.). *Hsi-tsang Fo-chiao I-shu* (Tibetan Buddhist Art). Peking, 1957.

KHANDALAWALA, K. "Some Nepalese and Tibetan Bronzes in the Collection of Mr. R. S. Sethna of Bombay," *Marg*, IV, 1 (1951), pp. 21–40.

———. "Masterpieces in South Indian and Nepalese Bronzes in the Collection of Mr. S. K. Bhedwar, Bombay," *Marg*, IV, 4 (1951), pp. 8–27.

KRAMRISCH, S. "Nepalese Paintings," *Journal of the Indian Society of Oriental Art*, I, 1 (1933), pp. 129–147.

———. "Art of Nepal and Tibet," *Philadelphia Museum of Art Bulletin*, 55, no. 265 (Spring 1960), pp. 23–28.

———. *The Art of Nepal*, New York, 1964.

———. "The Art of Nepal," *Oriental Art*, n.s. X, 4 (Winter 1964), pp. 225–233.

LANDON, P. *Nepal*. London, 1928.

LEVI, S. *Le Nepal*. 3 vols., Paris, 1905–08.

LIPPE, A. "Viṣṇu's Conch in Nepal," *Oriental Art*, n.s. VIII, 3 (Autumn 1962), pp. 117–119 and n.s. IX, 1 (Spring 1963), p. 47.

LOBSIGER-DELLENBACH, M. *Nepal: Catalogue de la Collection du Musée de Genève*. Geneva, 1954.

Nepalese Art, Kathmandu, 1966.

PAL, P. "Two Images of Mahāśri Tārā," *Proceedings of the Indian History Congress*. Trivandrum, 1948, pp. 137–141.

———. "Composite Form of Vāsudeva and Lakṣmī," *Journal of the Asiatic Society*, V, 3–4 (1952), pp. 73–80.

———. "Notes on Five Sculptures from Nepal," *British Museum Quarterly*, XXIX, 1 (1964–65), pp. 29–34.

———. "Vaiṣṇava Art from Nepal in the Museum," *Boston Museum Bulletin*, LXV, 340 (1967), pp. 40–60.

———. "Umā-Maheśvara Theme in Nepali Sculpture," *Boston Museum Bulletin*, LXVI, 345 (1968), pp. 85–100.

———. *Vaiṣṇava Iconology in Nepal*. Calcutta, 1970.

———. *Indo-Asian Art from the John Gilmore Ford Collection*. Baltimore, 1971.

———. *The Arts of Nepal*, Vol. I: Sculpture. Leiden/Koln, 1974.

PAL, P. and BHATTACHARYYA, D. C. *The Astral Divinities of Nepal*. Varanasi, 1969.

PAL, P. and TSENG, H. C. *Lamaist Art: The Aesthetics of Harmony*. Boston, 1969.

PETECH, L. *Medieval History of Nepal*. Rome, 1958.

Pūrṇima, Kathmandu, (quarterly, 1956 to date).

REGMI, D. R. *Ancient Nepal*. Calcutta, 1960.

———. *Medieval Nepal*. 3 vols., Calcutta, 1965–66.

SINGH, M. *Himalayan Art*. Greenwich, Conn., 1968.

SLUSSER, M. "Nepali Sculptures—New Discoveries," *Aspects of Indian Art* (ed. P. Pal), Leiden, 1972.

SLUSSER, M., and VAJRACHARYA, G. "Some Nepalese Stone Sculptures: A Reappraisal Within Their Cultural and Historical Context," *Artibus Asiae*, XXXV, 1/2, pp. 79–138.

SNELLGROVE, D. *Buddhist Himalaya*, Oxford, 1957.

———. "Shrines and Temples of Nepal," *Arts Asiatiques*, VIII, 1 and 2 (1961), pp. 3–10 and pp. 93–120.

TUCCI, G. *Preliminary Report on Two Scientific Expeditions in Nepal*. Rome, 1956.

———. *Nepal: The Discovery of the Malla*. London, 1962.

WALDSCHMIDT, E. and R. L. *Nepal: Art Treasures from the Himalayas*. New York, 1970.

Catalogue designed by Joseph Bourke Del Valle
Composition by A. Colish, Inc., Mount Vernon, N. Y.
Production supervised by John Weatherhill, Inc., New York and Tokyo
Printed in gravure and lithography by Nissha Printing Co. Ltd., Kyoto

PHOTOGRAPHS. William Abbenseth: 50; Phillip Allen: 13; Imants Anseergs: 4; Armen: 83; Blakeslee-Lane Inc.: 34, 57 (color), 92; Ferdinand Boesch: 15; Michael Budrys: 71; The Cleveland Museum of Art: 6, 22, 40 (color), 73; Edward Cornachio: 3, 5, 8, 9, 10, 23, 24, 32 (color), 39, 42, 44, 55, 59, 60, 61, 62, 64, 65, 70, 77, 80, 81, 82, 85, 89, 90, 93, 97 (color); Graphic Production Associates Inc.: 52, 94; Helga Photo Studios: 43 (color), 46; Dennis J. Iannarelli: 12, 31, 45, 51 (color), 95; Paul Macapia: 7, 16; Eugene Mantie: 19; James Medley: 75; D. C. Millard: 49, 78; Museum of Fine Arts, Boston: 48, 76; Otto Nelson: 1, 14 (color), 17, 18, 21, 25, 28 (color), 29 (color), 33, 35, 36, 47, 54, 58, 67, 68, 69, 72, 79, 86, 87 (color), 91; Eric Pollitzer: 26, 74; William Pons: 38; Lloyd W. Rule: 96; Jack Savage: 88; Duane Suter: 20, 27, 56, 84; Taylor & Dull, Inc.: 41; James Ufford: 11, 66; Charles Uht: 63; William H. Wolff: 2, 37.